W. H. Pomeroy,

Springfield,

Mass.

Augt 1873.

Bought by
A. W. Lawson
in Hartford Conn
April 1st 1916

THE DRAMA
OF EARTH.

THE

DRAMA OF EARTH.

BY

JEROME KIDDER.

NEW YORK:
PUBLISHED BY ADOLPHUS RANNEY,
195 BROADWAY.
1857.

SAVAGE & McCREA, STEREOTYPERS,
13 Chambers Street, N. Y.

PROLEGOMENA.

I BOW respectfully, and offer this book to the public, which, I hope, will discover a better reason for its appearance than any involving the partial presumption that it may have been determined by the ancient remark, that, "of making many books there is no end." What I have written, I have written, for which, I know not that there is any occasion consenting to the propriety of my offering apology or excuse. While it has been my object to show in what way human depravity is the result of the violation of the law of man's purest and highest being, it has been my object also to show that the minds of many, while considering human sufferings, often follow in a direction that leads away from the greatest evils, to those which, in comparison, are almost imaginary, and, however evil, yet the result of causes which are too little recognized.

I could have chosen a more pleasant theme; for it is more agreeable to consider man's virtues rather than his vices; to reflect on good rather than evil—pleasure rather than pain—happiness rather than misery; I would look on the pleasing phases of society rather than the repulsive—the sunny side of life rather than that which is palled with miserable night: but, inasmuch as evils of the greatest magnitude present themselves unlooked for, it may be well for any one to attempt to direct public attention to them, in order to effect, at least, their partial alleviation, whether in such attempt he should succeed or fail.

I have chosen to give this composition the form of a drama; yet it is not necessary for me to say that it is not intended for the stage. The reader will perceive that the feature of this drama, at the beginning, was suggested by portions of "Milton's Paradise Lost;" and though the whole may present features of fiction, yet it is intended to be founded on Divine revelations, truths of history, and facts to which the present generation is witness.

Placing this book before the American people, I will be allowed to express the conviction that to be a *true* American, a *true* Democrat, or a *true* Republican, is one; and when the spirit of such one prays, the chief burthen of that prayer, beyond what regards the expansion and continual happiness of his immortal being and the best welfare of his immediate friends, will be for his beloved country; and his country is not merely the town, nor the county, nor the state, in which he was born; nor the east, nor the west, nor the north, nor the south — but the whole east,and west, and north,and south,of this indissoluble compact of states. Let peace and prosperity attend its course, and its inhabitants be elevated in humanity — to which end, may it become free from the curse of intemperance, which the proof of history shows to be all-sufficient to bring any country down into ruin: let all its people be nourished into the highest and noblest life by the purity of virtue and the crystal waters in which are mingled no miseries; no widow's nor orphan's tears; no poisons for the body and the soul. The sound that comes from the crystal cascade,is not the lamentation of the bereaved; it is not the sighs of wretchedness and want; it is not the expression of delirious agonies; it is not the wailing of despair from immortal spirits! It is the music of joy — of peace; it is the song of love which may echo in the human heart, and be the accentuation that accords with the word of life and the harmony of heaven.

Spirit of Truth, if thou hast power to move
The blinded world aright, now guide my hand;
For by thy power I would essay to prove
The force which yet lies in the first command:
Though I would nothing now to earth reveal,
Yet I should dip my pen in liquid fire,
And write upon men's hearts that they may FEEL
The argument my being doth inspire—
To move the ponderous theme at my desire.

DRAMATIS PERSONÆ.

CHRIST, *the Savior.*

URIEL,
ITHURIEL,
and others, } *Holy Angels.*

LUCIFER,
BEELZEBUB,
DIABOLOS,
MAMMON,
TYPHON,
BACCHO,
IMP, } *Apostate Angels.*

ADAM,
EVE, } *First human pair.*

CAIN,
ABEL, } *Sons to* ADAM *and* EVE.

NOAH, *Builder of the Ark.*

SHEM,
HAM,
JAPHETH, } *Sons to* NOAH.

HEROD, *King of Judea.*

COLUMBUS, *a Mariner.*

LEGREE, *a Lawyer; afterward a Planter.*

CELESTRA, *Wife to* LEGREE.

Child, Daughter to LEGREE *and* CELESTRA.

BRIDGET, *Servant to* CELESTRA.

CASSY, EMELINE, } *Slaves to* LEGREE.

ST. CLARE, *a Planter.*

Friend of ST. CLARE *and* LEGREE.

MALVERTON, *formerly a Classmate with* LEGREE.

IAGO, CASSIO, } *Characters represented in the Play of* OTHELLO, *the Moor of Venice.*

Pilot of a Flat-boat—a Whisky-Dealer.

STOKES, *a Flat-boatman.*

SMOLLICK, *a regular Loafer.*

UNCLE TOM, *a Slave to* LEGREE.

QUIMBO, *Slave to* LEGREE, *and Slave-Overseer.*

RUMBLOSSOM, *an Insurgent.*

A Valet, southern Gentlemen, northern Gentleman, Woman, Marshal, Officers, Soldiers, Citizens, Boatswain, Sailors, Distiller, Servant, Landlords, Insurrectionists, Whisky-Inspector, Land-Pirates, Ticket-seller of the Notional Theatre, &c.

THE DRAMA OF EARTH.

SCENE I.

A dark Abyss. — LUCIFER *and* BEELZEBUB *discovered in the Mists.*

BEEL. It IS so! Heaven is lost! Those realms of light
Remain to those who, with victorious might,
Urged back rebellion —
LUC. That had nigh usurped
Entire dominion. We have fled beyond
Heaven's domination —
BEEL. Into deepest wo! —
Those blest retreats and those delightful vales,
Did echo with celestial melodies,
Till martial strains, athwart the harmony,
Broke the soft cadence, setting all astir;
And the result hath been our overthrow
Into this dark and horrible abyss,

Beyond the tone of peace or other sound,
Except the wail of deepest agonies,
And raging of these fiery elements.
Is all for ever lost? Must we abide
Our sad reverses in this punishment?
Must we endure this torturous extreme;
For Heaven's afflictive wrath pursues us here?

LUC. Be it not ever thus: What if I charge
These fulminating lightnings too with wrath,
With which we may assail heaven's fast-barred gates,
And wage subversive violence beyond?
And if we thus reverse the fate of war—
And if we thus regain our native heaven—
And if we thus dethrone heaven's ancient King—
And if we thus—

BEEL. O these unhappy ifs,
Forebode reverses we might further feel,
And fill with dread the vast uncertainty.
When raged the warfare, all our gathered strength
In phalanx, an innumerable host,
Thy purpose seconded with fierce array,
And thou didst lead them all embattled, swift
On into combat! Then all heaven shook
With hostile clamor as th' opposing hosts
Of cherubim and seraphim arranged
Imposing on our front, contended hard

With might that dared defy Omnipotence;
For we have learned, though we have learned too late,
He is Omnipotent who reigns in heaven.
Long time the even strife of battle raged,
Until the Son, with potent arm aloft,
Held forth a shield from which transcendent light
Flashed swift and fierce across the empyrean,
Breaking its awful volleys on our hosts,
Who fled amazed, confounded, and repulsed;
And through heaven's walls that oped for us a way,
With tempests from his armory, pursued
Into this outer deep, where yet his wrath,
Lingering, abides, and now awakes these torments!
Is it not vain to use our hostile arms
Against such armor, and wage open war
'Gainst such a foe?

LUC. It will behoove us rather,
To vex, as best we can, the powers of heaven,
But not assail where sure defeat awaits
With deeper vengeance on our vanquished hosts;
Though we are vanquished, we are not subdued —
No, an immortal hate lives in us still;
And yet our foes shall feel its influence.
I know that God is the Omnipotent:
The throne whereon he sits, eternally
Belongs to him, and any power beside

Need not dispute heaven's empire with its King,
Who, from the womb of Chaos, doth evoke
Innumerable worlds. Now wily thoughts
Inspire me. I will quickly venture forth
Into those vasty depths: what if he make
Of that consistence in which Chaos reigns,
A world where I shall be?

BEEL. What wouldst thou do?
Would purposed effort serve thy doing much?
Its inward portion wouldst thou melt with fire,
And from its opening sides spout flaming horrors?
And while the angels yet around the throne,
Sing hallelujahs loud to their Creator,
Wouldst thou wake howlings in that world, and shout
Such noises as would fright the empyrean —
Or aught that would the least advantage us?

LUC. If chance direct me so that world shall be
The one on which will dwell the habitants
Of whom much ancient rumor did foretell —
Since out of heaven's gates we have been hurled
Into this dread abyss of punishment,
The tricks that I shall play upon the world
Will startle Heaven with astonishment.

BEEL. O, will they so? That would be some return
For these afflictions.

LUC. It would be some return!—
It would be great return for these afflictions.
BEEL. This shall not always be our habitation,
Immured with God's immitigable wrath.
LUC. Though it be not, 't is better here to wait
Awhile among these woes, than serve in heaven.
BEEL. For that there may be no alternative.
LUC. Beelzebub, thou hast attended me,
And learned thereby of my intended way
To Chaos' depths, where I shall seek of chance,
Direction to that portion of her realm,
Which being touched by the creative Power
Shall change into a world whereon shall dwell
Embodied spirits — Godlike images —
Of whom prophetic rumor long ago
Was heard in heaven. Ere I thither go,
Receive my mandate; keep the strictest watch
Along the confines of these angry floods,
Lest some escape, reluctant to abide
With us the issues of an adverse war;
And thus escaped, pursue their wandering course
Through Chaos, till the scouts sent out from heaven,
Espy them, then with searching eye pursue
The darksome vastness wherein I shall lurk,
And there discovering me, turn swift their flight
Back to the empyrean, and acquaint

Th' Avenger that he stretch his mighty arm,
And snatch us quickly out the frightened deep
Of dark consistence, then to deeper woes
In blackest hell, fling us precipitant.
My mandate is delivered, and beware.

BEEL. 'T is said: Thy mandate shall be my regard:
But why strict watch? Can any find a way
Out this abysm? I doubt if thou thyself
Canst make thy strength of such avail; for see
What walls of adamantine darkness bound
This place of torment: Dost thou think to pass
Through such, and find thy pathway safe beyond?

LUC. I do, and with these tangled lightnings, I
Will pass through the cleft darkness; there is none
Of all these hosts that followed us beyond
Dominion of the Throne, superior
To thee, and therefore thou mayst reign as prince.
I shall return to this abode again,
When I have learned how to enlarge thy reign.

[EXIT LUCIFER, *breaking his way through the darkness with lightnings.*

BEEL. The prince of all
In this abode,
Where woes appal
The rebel brood,

I can abide
Those torments sore,
And I will chide
No more.

DIABOLOS *rises through the dark mists*

DIAB. 'Tis wo's extreme to tread this angry lake,
Where fiery tempests ride the murky air,
And volleyed thunder's heavy movements break
On night extinguishing the ligntning's glare,
While from these torments, hideous howlings wake
Within this concave echoes of despair!
BEEL. Thinkst thou that this is the extreme of wo?
DIAB. What dost thou think? To be for ever here
And suffer vengeance? Say, canst thou endure
All this?
BEEL. I can endure all this and more;
What though th' Avenger hurl upon our heads
All vaster torments, still I could endure
The fierce addition; for there yet is hope
That there will come a respite from these woes.
DIAB. That such may be I can not comprehend.
Will hurling down destruction weary Him,
The Omnipotent, who drove us out of heaven,
And thus come slackened vengeance? or thinkst thou
This punishment will tame us to submission

So that his wrath be quiet? Thou dost know
We could not serve in heaven, and therefore comes
This dread infliction.

BEEL. If the will rebel
Against strict fate, it makes itself a hell:
To this endurance let the will accord
Until the future show how we may turn
Regard upon the vexed Creation yet.

DIAB. Creation: Ay, I know thou meanest much;
Yet can we hinder the creative Power,
Or mar a portion of his work, thinkst thou?
If so, when may it have accomplishment?

BEEL. I can not tell thee now, though well I know
The future doth reserve advantages
For us, and these, unlooked for, when they come,
May startle heaven's triumphant warriors.

DIAB. The present we know well and can not choose,
Although we rather would be ignorant
Of that we be, and of this sufferance,
Yet why, if shadows of the future come
To do thee service, didst thou take up arms
Against th' Omnipotent, and not foresee
Thyself and all these legions hurled beyond
Heaven's confines, and beyond the bounds of light,
Into this utter darkness—canst thou tell

So much about the past I fain would know?

BEEL. The past is past, and subject to no change:
Therefore turn not reflections on the past,
But rather turn thy hopes upon the future
That may bring change to this unhappy durance—
For to this end has Lucifer gone hence,
And me appointed prince in this abysm.

DIAB. He gone? I had not thought it possible
That even the mightiest could make his way
Through these vast walls of adamantine night,
That do surround this depth of misery.
Then why may we not follow, and escape
These punishments?

BEEL. Nay, I have charge to watch
That none from this dark prison shall escape,
Lest at imprudent time there should go forth
These legions to th' espy of scouts from heaven,
And thus bring on us vengeance multiplied.

DIAB. Does he thus first attempt the desert void,
And there to deviate through darkest space,
Or search the crude consistence whereof worlds
Innumerable are made, that he may hide
From the Almighty's vengeance—he, the first
Who did insinuate among these hosts
Hapless rebellion—does he now command
That none else flee beyond Heaven's wrath inflict,

Lest numbers should betray to Heaven's watch,
Yet thinking there himself safe, where no eye
Of Heaven's vigilance can search him out—
He that did lead us into direst conflict,
And overthrow into this dreadful deep?

BEEL. Beyond these walls, but not from punishment,
Hath he escaped; for yet Heaven's wrath inflicts
Enduring woes within him, and himself
Is ever his own hell, as we our own—
Although we curse these fiery elements
That strive tempestuous. He now doth tread,
Afar beyond these walls, the solitude
Of ancient Chaos, which creative Power
Molds into worlds, and in their circling ways
Sets periods continual of time. There Lucifer has gone.
What thinkst thou if his espionage search out,
Some part the universe, the mystery
Of the creation, and, by prudent wiles,
Vex the Creator sorely by pursuing
With vast destruction the ultimity
Of all his works?

DIAB. I wish it may be done;
For such revenge would lessen much our woes.

BEEL. And such may be our reasonable hope.

DIAB. A hope that will present us present cheer.

IMP *appears through the dark mist.*

IMP. I wish I were in heaven again, gathering
Sweet dews, breathing the balms, and listening
To best music of harps, which I can not
Hear now in this dark place of torments; but
In this most hot and smoky place I hear
Lamenting noise, which I help make! I wish
I were in heaven again.——

BEEL. If thou dost wish such wishes, thou mayst wish
Till thou shalt wish that wishing wishes thus
Could bring thy wish. I tell thee, wishing Imp,
If thou dost have such wishes in thy thoughts,
It will be better not to utter them.

IMP. More wishes thou hast uttered even now
Than I have.

BEEL. Tempt me not to do thee harm,
Or I will make thee wish thou couldst not speak.

IMP. Thou canst not do more harm to me than I
Feel now: I will get out of this bad place.

BEEL. Wilt thou? ha! wilt thou? I tell thee, Imp,
That thou canst not; and if thou shouldst attempt,
I will bind thee with lightnings, and cast thee down
Into the uttermost deep, and pile on thee
Mountains of melting adamant! Aha!
There thou shalt ever strive in vain to give
To discontent a partial utterance.

IMP. Oh! oh! I will not try to get away,
And I will do whatever thou require.

BEEL. And wilt thou ever do what I require?

IMP. Ever, Master, if it be in my power.

BEEL. Thou shalt; and let thy disaffection cease
From audible expression; so shalt thou,
With experiment, find what is best.

IMP. That I have done: what is there more that thou
Wilt have me do? I'll do it quickliest.

BEEL. Thou mayst wander through these sulphurous mists,
Which will affect thee with a change, and make
Obedience, result of willingness:
Naught further yet—and yet the future may
Bring much to be accomplished by thy aid.

IMP. I go, Master—I go my way through fire,
And smoke, and noises; for I must obey. [*Exit* IMP.

BEEL. Imp was the youngest of the warring host,
And hesitated whether he should join
Our forces in the conflict, when all heaven
Jarred heavy with the clash of armories—
And lingered last of all who thence were driven;
And palest fear attended his dire way.

DIAB. Although so young, and slow in choice, yet wise
Perhaps as we, who, choosing quickly, chose
The cause that brought upon us all this ill.

BEEL. 'Tis done beyond all hope or thought of
change,
Except such change as gratifies revenge;
Therefore our business will be yet to do
What comes in range of our vindictive power.
Is not ambition now half satisfied?
We know our strength; before, we knew it not:
And what if knowledge be so dearly bought?—
'Tis better thus by far than not to know.
Here will we wander through these wrathful fires,
Contriving mischief until Lucifer
Shall make return from his adventure far;
Then may we know how we can bring our hate
To bear effective 'gainst creative Might! [*Exeunt.*

SCENE II.

EDEN.—*Enter* LUCIFER.

LUCIFER. This world from chaos rolled, at His command
Who rules in the creation as in heaven,
Where I could never reign; yet in this world
I will set up my everlasting kingdom,
If it avail me aught that I reign here.
These beasts of many kinds, fowls of the air,
And finny tribes that move among the floods,
Which the Creator made to suit his pleasure,
Are not of my regard save to destroy:
Should I destroy them it would suit my pleasure,
If there be none of higher order here,
On whom to wreak revenge for all our woes:—
But what is he who walks the earth erect,
Whose brow is throned reason, and his bearing
So like an angel—rather like a God!
Creation's ultimate—the counterpart
Of the creative Prototype!—The beasts

Around him fawn and do him reverence,
And there submissively await him lord.
He seems the object of Heaven's chief regard,
And hence he is the object of my hate.
I further see he is accompanied
By one, his like, yet of a softer mold.
To them alone, upon this world is given,
Thought's interchange by speech. Are they not Gods?
Who have such bearing, and whose images
Show such an impress of intelligence,
Where reason is the umpire? Are they Gods?
Together they make casual approach,
And I will be invisible among
These comprehending shades, and hear their converse.

Enter Adam *and* Eve.

Eve. O how much happiness it is to be
Where Heaven's favors are so bountiful
That they administer to all our wants!

Adam. Not only to be here among these bounties
Of pleasing prospects and delicious fruits,
But to be here with *thee*, my loved companion,
Is all the fullness of my earthly bliss.

Eve. When thou art happy, I am happy too—
So much thy joys administer to mine;
And thus I think it will for ever be.

ADAM. It will be ever thus, if we obey
As willing subjects to the will of Heaven.
Thou seest all these beasts which we have named,
Do fawn obsequious; we are lords of them,
And they obey us; they yield not in strength:
'Tis the superiority of mind
That holds them willing in submission now.
Our reason's tenure is conditional,
Which with its normal influence directs
Our actions that we do no being wrong,
But have a love for all that God has made;
And then the soul exists in purity.
If no extraneous and rebellious essence
Mix with the salient currents of the life,
Then will our beings ever thus remain
In harmony with all the universe,
And the Creator of the universe.

EVE. And is there danger that our reason be,
By some rebellious essence, overcome,
So that, from its abnormal influence,
We would regard not universal good?

ADAM. O Eve, there is an interdicted tree
In th' midst of this fair garden, which, if we
Partake of, dreadful ill will come upon us:
And passing near, no doubt thou hast observed
Its branches reaching far on every side;

And specious is its fruit; but if we taste,
Or even touch it, we will surely die!
EVE. And yet I can not comprehend what death
We would incur by eating of that fruit.
Would these our bodies, in the self-same day,
Cease to exist, and be entirely nothing?
Or can the meaning be, death of the soul?
I rather think the soul will never die,
But will live on, and on, and on, forever.
ADAM. We would not cease to be, but cease to bear
The image of our Archetype divine.
That fruit has such pernicious quality,
It would contaminate the fluid life,
That, from the fountain, does its offices
To the whole system; and the mind would be
Dragged down in deepest darkness, destitute
Of thoughts of heaven and eternity;
And on the very earth—below the earth—
Even lower than the beasts—our grovelling thoughts
Would course in deep and dire depravity.
EVE. O partner of my joys! who taught thee thus?
ADAM. A short time since, even when thou wast created,
Which time I slept, came dreams, with sights and sounds
That waked my soul. Anon an angel came

From the bright regions just beyond the sky,
Which opened as he passed, who turned his flight
Down into Paradise, and over me
Made sudden pause, with admonition thus:—
"Adam, attend; thy Maker will command."
Anon a voice out of the empyrean,
Came down in soft, commanding cadences:—
"Of every tree of th' garden thou mayst eat;
But of the tree of th' knowledge of good and evil,
Thou shalt not eat of it; for in the day
Thereof thou eatest, thou shalt surely die!"
O Eve, great then was my anxiety,
And fearful my misgivings; but anon,
The angel did instruct and comfort me,
Admonishing obedience to Heaven,
As I have since advised. Eve, thou hast heard:
My dear companion, let us e'er be wary.
The orb of day now stoops before the night;
Let us go, therefore, to our couch of rest.

[*Exeunt* ADAM *and* EVE.

LUC. Go; and ere long a living death await you,
And everlasting anguish be your rest!
There is no secret out of heaven—none
That serves not espionage. My legions vast,
That are imprisoned far in vaster night,
I shall bring hither for no little cause:

Beelzebub, whom I appointed prince
In the complaining deep, to ease the wounds
Which his expectancy had erst received
By dire expulsion from the realms of light,
With his auxiliar service here will serve me;
And all that there bewail their miseries,
Let forth from wrathful night, shall hither come,
And find a respite doing mischief here!
I will haste thither—heaven's gate is shut;
The day descends, and shade lies on my way;
But yonder, as from heaven, now Uriel
Bears hitherward, and light attends his way;
I know him well, for once we closely met
In conflict, but it now must be my care
That he shall not know me, nor whence I am;
No doubt I can learn much to my advantage,
If I await his coming and appear
An angel as from heaven immediate—
Now with the semblance of supernal sheen,
I will dissemble so that afterward,
Myself will marvel when I think of it.

Enter URIEL.

I saw thee [*to* URIEL], when thy bright and airy way
Turned hitherward across the evening mists.
Admiring all the works of the Creator,
As I, thou too, perhaps, hast hither come,

Down from th' empyreal regions to behold,
With an exploring eye, this happy world.
What joy it is to chant in heaven the praise
Of Him who hath created the blest spirits
In heaven adoring, and the many orbs
In the immensity: what joy to swell
The song loud and afar, and hear the choir
Of vast creation all in chorus join,
And tongues celestial chime the interlude
Of cadences among the rolling spheres.

URIEL. To Him all praise belongs: To Him all heaven
Attune symphonious songs, while all His works
Accord soft harmonies.

LUC. Verily, hast thou,
While in thy wanderings, visited the orbs
Circling the day, or far beyond the light
That flows effulgent here, even in the vast
Which the creation fills, found other worlds
That, more than this, partake of heaven's regard,
Where beings dwell, highest in excellence
Of any that inhabit them?

URIEL. None more than this;
For here the habitation is of MAN,
The highest of intelligences that[1]
Inhabit any orb, of whom the fame

Went forth prophetic 'mong the heavenly hosts,
Long time before the mighty King did wage,
Against arrayed rebellion, dreadful war,
When all his enemies were overthrown,
And cast out into darkness — into wo!

LUC. A loss much felt in heaven when suddenly,
So many legions left their sighing harps
Strewed thickly over heaven's broad champaign!

URIEL. Th' extreme necessity that did compel
The swift expulsion thence, did not prevent
Commiseration for the dire distress
Of heaven's lost legions, whose sad harps — attuned,
In their last touch, to the according praise
That rang symphonious through the empyrean —
Sighed forth their lingering tones in lamentation,
And mournful grew the cadence, and more mournful,
Till drowned with din of hostile armaments;
And when the volleys of transcendent light
From the uplifted shield of Heaven's Son,
Broke on the serried ranks of rebel hosts,
And turned their flight beyond the walls of heaven —
The tempest even of solid light and flame,
That, swift pursuing, urged the lingering,
Sighed when the last of the rebellious angels
Fell out the opened walls; then turning back,
Resolving to ethereal again,

Sighed heavily along the empyrean.
Oh, then did the triumphant warriors
Weep sorrowful! Again the tempest sighed,
And sighing, to God's armory returned!
LUC. Does the victorious King of heaven fear,
Again will rise rebellion, that he keeps
His armories filled with the waiting tempests
Of latent light and flame that may again,
Should any exigency call them forth
To do the will of Might, burst into life,
And with destruction quickly overwhelm
Aspiring monarchies?
URIEL. He doth not fear
That more of his blest worshippers will fall
From their estate most happy, but 'tis known,
That he who first incited to rebellion—
Appollyon, premier of all motive ill,
Who, with his rash adherents, was cast forth
Into imprisoned darkness, hath made way
Beyond the bounds of that restricted night,
And may, with all his reckless votaries—
If he should work their way out that abysm—
Again attempt—O, vain would be th' attempt—
To overthrow heaven's ancient sovereignty;
And though he should not make such vain attempt,
No doubt he will essay to work his wiles

Among th' intelligences that inhabit
These new created orbs, and chiefly this,
Where MAN, Heaven's last and greatest work, abides,
Whom to estrange from Heaven, would bring joy
To the apostate Leader.

LUC. Ay, and throw
Echoes of laughter out th' abysm of wo!

URIEL. Yet to prevent such deprecated evil,
The universal Sovereign hath, my seat,
Set vigilant in the sun, from which I watch,
Observing if the Foe attempt encroachment
In these parts, so may providence avert
His purposed mischief.

LUC. Has thy wariness
Observed aught here suspicion doth regard,
That just at evening thou hast left thy seat
In th' sun, and come swift hither panoplied?
My stay before thy coming, had espied
None that may need thy watching, therefore grant,
It would be better—would it not be better,
If thou give not thy weary vigilance
And service to unnecessary care?

URIEL. I had observed such, and I tell thee that
Thy words as ill become thee as thy sheen,
Through which I now discover that thy shape
Hath dared appear in such a speciousness,

As for a time did hide designing ill.
Appollyon, false Dissembler, thou art he,
Who, ere declining day to evening's shades
Began to yield earth's paradise, I saw,
With volumed darkness hanging on his way,
Stride awkward down the mountain, out whose top
Belched clouds of smoke and flames and liquid fires.
Thy purpose here is to work ill. Away!
Lest fell destruction wait upon thy stay!

LUC. Ha, Uriel, lookst thou so,—ha, lookst thou so?
Thou knowst me then, and thou didst hither come
Upon a sunbeam from the luminous orb,
To spy me out, and thither mayst return;
And thou mayst hope, the eve being more advanced,
That quickly down that slanting beam of light,
Speed urge thee.

URIEL. Foe of heaven, who art thou
That darest by thy minatary voice,
As well as by thy evil purpose here,
Subject thyself to peril?

LUC. Thou knowst me,
Yet knowst me not; then know that I am he
Who led embattled legions into conflict
That shook the founded heavens, and did set
Pale terror on th' array of hostile foes;
And knowing this, if thou dost have regard

Now Uriel lifts aloft his flaming sword
And Lucifer flees from impending danger.

PAGE 33.

For thy own safety, let thy flight be quick.
URIEL. Audacious Fugitive, I know that thou
Didst lead thy legions all embattled on
To swift discomfiture and disarray;
Then thou and all thy vanquished warriors,
Through heaven's opened walls did quickly turn
Your flight precipitant in fearful haste,
Before descending storms of fiery hail,
While in advance awaking meteors glanced
In fitful mood, and glared with fitful blaze,
To light you on, and on, into the deep,
Where angry whirlwinds rushed to furious strife,
And dashed the liquid, elemental fire
On adamantine darkness that shrieked out
The echoes of your wailing miseries,
While lightnings fiercely flashed, and awing thunders
Rolled ponderous along th' abyss of wo!

[*Now* URIEL *lifts aloft his flaming sword,*
And LUCIFER *flees from impending danger —*
Just as an ostrich, when the Arab's horse
Pursues, half runs, half-flies, so on the earth,
He leaves the impress of his cloven foot,
And with his wings spread wide, and talons at
Th' extremes, with motion quick, both ran and flew.

In flight he safety seeks: his purpose here
Would work progressive ill. Night's mantle now
Hangs over paradise, and sleep, no doubt,
Has shut the world from man, save what through
dreams,
In image, is presented to his fancy.
I will at once attend him, and present
Such faithful reminiscence to his spirit—
Of Heaven's command, as deeply will impress
His waking hours; then will I turn my flight
Direct to heaven with all anxiety;
And all the powers empyreal shall learn
Recounted venture, and the Foe's design
Here to usurp supremacy, no doubt. [*Exit.*

SCENE III.

The dark Abyss.—Enter BEELZEBUB, DIABOLOS, MAMMON, TYPHON, IMP, *and* BACCHO.

DIAB. Long is the time that Lucifer hath left
Us here in wearisome uncertainty
Of his return from solitary way,
On which he dared essay the lonely waste,
Beyond this dark and dread imprisonment.

BEEL. Though long hath been the time, if well employed,
It is the best assurance of success;
Therefore, although his absence be prolonged,
That need not add to our uneasiness.

DIAB. Behold what fury agitates this gulf—
Behold the dark floods surging billowy;
Now fiercer lightnings strike upon these walls,
And the foundations of this concave shake!

BEEL. This is unwonted fury, and, no doubt,
Betokens the arrival of our chief:—
Behold the walls of darkness open now
To strokes of darting fire! Lo now, he comes!

Enter LUCIFER.

DIAB. Hail, Sovereign, Chief of all these many powers
That have awaited long thy welcome back!
BEEL. Hail, Chieftain, hail! The myriad of hosts,
Have waited anxiously, again to greet thee.
LUC. Hail, Prince, and all these warriors that fled
From domination, choosing rather wo
Than servitude in heaven!—would you know
What hopes lie out upon our distant way?
BEEL. Let all the vast deep be attentive now,
To learn of every peril or success
That hath awaited thee. No doubt some means
For opportune revenge, hath fallen on
Thy ventures: We would know what chances lie
Beyond this darkness; what discoveries
Where works the Ancient, and where is the image
Of the Creator, as foretold in heaven,
If any such hath been created yet!
LUC. When I had passed these walls, my doubtful way
Lay swift through solitudes of ancient night,
Where the creation, at remotest verge,
Encroached upon rude chaos, and forthwith,
The power of law controlled that part the wild
Which compassed me about, and voluble,

The huge concerted mass, detached, rolled forth
Into creation; and in circuit wide,
The rolling sphere pursued its steady round.
Its vast and ponderous circumference
Oppressed me, thus confined in central globe,
And there my struggles long attrite, did melt
That portion of the mass conglomerate,
Contiguous about me, all to fire—
To liquid fire! Anon I blew a blast
Of very flame, that out the earth shot far,
Making the convex gape. Through that hiatus,
The liquid welled, that cooled on the outside,
And formed a mountain, through whose opened top,
The like eruptions, oft successive poured
Adown its slopes. Up through the crater large,
My way proceeded, thence afar I viewed
The broad horizon, and with peering eye
Surveyed with care, the traveled orb around,
And found that animation held degrees,
Each in the special form that suited it;
But there was none with image like to God,
Discovered yet, and thence I turned my way
Back to the mountain, when I heard such sounds
As though the whole infinity of worlds,
Sung choruses, and all the sons of Heaven
Shouted for joy!

BEEL. It was not long ago,
Strange and mysterious sounds, of origin
From far, gave intonation audible
Above these thunders!

LUC. Doubtless 'twas the same.
Upon the next day, in the evening,[2]
Not long before the night:—for day and night
Move round the world successive as it turns
Its sides alternate to the central orb
That shades far light,—I trod again where shades
Of growing arbors, gathered on my way;
And while my vision turned with aspect sharp,
Through many separate ambrosial shades,
I saw two beings walking both erect,
Unlike all others, and discoursing oft
In happy conversance. They seemed like gods.
There will we go and gratify revenge
For heaven's afflictive vengeance.

BEEL. Let us bring
Upon him, quick destruction unawares,
And to this end, inhale the hottest flames,
That issue from the world's internal fires,
And blow athwart his way destruction dire,
And scatter all his being into nothing!
Thus ending the Creator's greatest work—
The creature uncreated suddenly!

Luc. Is to be ended greatest of all ills,
While in such end, one knows not he is ended,
And in such want of knowledge, ends all wo?
Had it been thus, we all would have been ended,
When we with haste fled quickly out of heaven.
Had we been ended, then we had escaped
The wrath that doth afflict our beings now;
Yet such impassively we can endure,
If we can bring on man a living death:
We will not end him, but will mar him so
That Heaven shall weep to look upon his wo.

Beel. We will not end him, but inflict such pain
Upon him, that revenge will be our gain.

Luc. Not further shall aggressive arms but wiles
More puissant, disarm the conqueror,
And into torments of the nether deep,
Betray the earth's God-like inhabitants.
I've tried the force of arms, and now will try
What force in deepest subtilty doth lie.

Beel. I've tried the force of arms and now will see
If there be greater force in subtilty.

Diab. The greatest force that is in arms I've tried:
I'll prove if more in subtilty abide.

Typhon. I've tried the force of arms, and soon can tell
If greater force in subtilty doth dwell.

MAM. I've tried the force of arms, and fled amain,
Yet subtilty may turn my loss to gain.

IMP. My arms did little, and I fain would be
Where I could try the power of subtilty.

BAC. We tried the force of arms and quick defeat
Drove us forth quickly out of heaven, yet relying on
subtile stimulant our warfare we will repeat.

LUC. Now all ye powers, once overcome in fight,
But not subdued, and able to confound
Your mighty foes with dread, who are no doubt
Susceptible of it, prepare to go
A journey swift and far out from this deep,
Into that world where machinations shall
Serve our severest purpose, till alarm
Find heaven, no doubt unconscious of what ill
Is hatched in hell, to bear upon mankind
Respected with heaven's vigilance so much,
That wariness behooves us; for the angels,
No doubt, tend thither with oft ministrations;
Indeed I did encounter one of them —
'Twas Uriel, and since but he, I thought
It hardly worth the while to drive him thence.
Our course will be directly to the vent
Whence issue liquid fires; not such as these,
Fierce in enduring age, but such as are
Congenial rather to our habitudes;

Then will we go and come, and on the earth,
Make havoc as will suit convenience quite.
Seize now these lightnings! all ye mighty hosts,
And with them, break these walls of adamant,
And here no more will be our weary stay,
And we will find revenge upon our way!

[With multiplying strokes of lightnings fierce,
Th' Infernal hosts unite in one essay,
Not vain; for strokes on strokes, redoubled, pierce
The prison walls which suddenly give way,
And let them forth; and in complete array,
Toward earth direct, they swift pursue their flight,
Where they arrive just at the close of day;
And thicker darkness spreads far on the night,
While round the mountain's smoking crater they alight.

SCENE IV.

A Volcano.—*Enter* LUCIFER *and* BEELZEBUB.

BEEL. Here is so much I know so little of,
That for inquiries, may excuses plead:
What place was that we crossed, so very fair?
And what or who was that that stood erect,
Majestically there surveying all?
LUC. All that, respecting which thou dost inquire,
Pertains in common to our interests—
And ceremonial apology
Need not precede. That place was paradise,
And that was MAN, who held thy passing glance
Of admiration—there erect, supreme
Among those willing animals that wait
His ruling gait and his commanding voice.
When hitherward from the deep night of hell,
Our way crossed that elysium, ere the day
Had quite withdrawn for night's approaching shades,
Those arbors of thy wonder and those fruits,
Bright in the gleaming sun, were all for man—

The arbors to protect him from the heat
Of the meridian day; those fruits his food
On which his life depends continually.
The quality of fruit which he partakes,
Will qualify his nature. In that garden
There is a tree of Heaven's interdiction,
Whose fruit, if he partake, its quality
Will bring destruction even on his being.

BEEL. O, I perceive that, by thy journey here,
Thy espionage has not been vain at all,
Since such important secret is discovered,
And by whatever means it matters not.

LUC. From Adam's converse with his consort Eve,
Which I had overheard, this I did learn,
Which knowledge from an angel he received,
To answer every question of his thought,
Thus with philosophy of Nature's law—
If in the salient currents of the life
Mix no extraneous or rebellious essence
Then his pure spirit ever will remain
In harmony with all the laws of heaven.

BEEL. In making noxious essence, Heaven did work
To our advantage, if the interdict
Shall be unheeded, which shall be our care.

LUC. What Heaven lacked in doing, we shall do;
What we do will not be the work of Heaven;

And when we shall have caused the fall of man,
Our triumph will be great, and greater far,
If man so fallen, charge 'gainst heaven his fall!
BEEL. As day and night alternate move around
This rolling earth that circles far the sun,
I think yon grey betokens morning near;
And will it not be well, when day shall dawn,
That thou, or I, or both of us, should go,
And lead him in temptation, that he eat
The evil fruit, and therefore be destroyed?
LUC. Soon as the coming day begins its course,
I will in paradise attempt man's fall;
But thither, I will Baccho send at once,
To bring a portion of the evil fruit;
For I suspect its quality is such,
I may observe its curious effects.
BEEL. Baccho, with the remainder of our hosts,
Is in the central globe, which way this wide
Hiatus leads, through which rise smoke and flames.
LUC. Upon my summons he will quickly come.
Ho, Baccho, let thy presence here attend.

Enter BACCHO.

BACCHO. Great Master, here I am; what shall I do?
LUC. Observe yon garden with its many trees;
And central, there is one with branches far

Extended, bearing very specious fruit.
Go thither on thy momentary way,
And of its fruit bring hither specimen,
With the electric speed of thy return.

BACCHO. I will; It shall be brought here quickliest;
Even now I smell its goodly quality. [*Exit* BACCHO.

LUC. No doubt that Baccho, though inferior
To most that fled from high dominion, will
Be instrument effecting very much
That through our hopes, lie in the future yet.

BEEL. Perhaps, though now I can not judge of it.

Enter BACCHO *with fruit.*

BACCHO. Here is the fruit: those ails be gone so there be ease in me, and forgetfulness of the afflictive punishments. That garden be mine; this world be mine; all the planets be mine; all the universe be mine, and I be the King of it. Go to! go to! I can rend ye with thunderbolts, and tempests of flame, and fiery hail! I can rend the earth! I can blast creation!

LUC. He has partaken of the evil fruit,
And manifests its visible effects;
And with it now his habitude conforms;
And in conformity thereof will he
Pursue on earth, abounding influence.

Now take him into the interior globe
Through the hiatus yawning wide near by.
[*Exit* BEELZEBUB *with* BACCHO.
The orb of day is rising now, and morn,
From orient, is crossing paradise,
Where I shall quick repair to work man's fall. [*Exit.*

SCENE V.

EDEN.—*Enter* EVE, *gathering fruits.*

EVE. Sleep lingers on him still, and he may rest
From yesterday's fatigue attending on
His labor here among these fruitful trees;[3]
For I would rather that he still repose—
And yet I choose not to be here alone.

Enter ADAM.

ADAM. Eve, my beloved, my ever dear companion,
Thy absence from my side hath wakened me;
And I have sought thee, though not long have sought,
And found thee here.
EVE. Yea, I am gathering fruits,
Of which our banquet will be soon prepared,
And we together will enjoy repast

Of all delicious fruits — none that would harm:
But something I have reminiscence of,
That doth impress me sadly.

ADAM. What it is,
I fain would know, because my happiness
Increases or diminishes with thine:
I apprehend that thou hast been advised
In dreams again, as I, what danger from
Heaven's Enemy may yet beset us here.

EVE. Thou dost presume correctly; for last night—
Even as the night before, concerning which
I gave some intimation yesterday—
While I was sleeping, dreams awaked my soul,
Which with an angel from the realms above,
Held converse; and he counseled me that I
With care avoid the interdicted fruit.
Then I did greatly wonder what the cause
Of so much fear that we would disobey;
And by inquiry learned some evil spirit—
The chief of many legions which with him,
For disobedience, were driven from heaven,
And mured in depths of adamantine night—
Had fled imprisonment, and hitherward
Turned his designing way, and would, no doubt,
From motives of revenge, essay to bring
Upon us all destructive influence.

ADAM. While we obey, no harm can come upon us;
So there need not be fear, save it be fear
That we shall disobey by eating of
The interdicted tree, and there is no
Necessity for that, since here we find
All fruits that are essential to supply
Our wasting bodies, which to Nature's law
Are subjects of accordance, and must yield
To a continual change, though it will bring
Our dissolution and return to dust,
Of which we are composed.

EVE. Yea, we shall die,
Though we eat not the interdicted fruit.

ADAM. Our bodies must; all matter organized,
Must pass to dissolution; all that grow —
Yea, all that, by their circulating life,
Continually change their particles,
Until it brings the sure effect of death:
So every plant, and every shrub and tree;
All beasts, all birds, all tribes that live in waters;
All that are formed of dust, to dust return:
But Oh that other death which we would die,
If we should eat of that forbidden tree —
A living death! an everlasting death!

EVE. I know not that I fully comprehend
The living death, the everlasting death,

Which we would find in disobedience.

ADAM. By th' evil fruit our beings would be marred,
Nor be like the creative Prototype;
And low and vile would be our thoughts and deeds:
And it would hasten dissolution too,
Of this organic temple of the soul;
And when this body yields to dissolution,
Oh! then the soul—so far estranged from God,
And cast into perdition, only fit
For company with Heaven's rebellious foes—
Would range for ever in consuming wrath,
And never be consumed, but vainly wish
Annihilation! Such would even be
The living death—the everlasting death!
O Eve! we now enjoy terrestrial bliss,
And naught will mar our happiness, if we
Shall faithfully regard the interdict
Which has been given for purpose positive,
And not to make a trial of our will;
For the Omniscient hath no need to make
Experiment, to know with how much power
He hath ordained us! Here we may partake
The fruit craved by our normal appetites;
And hitherto, on our sufficient food,
We have subsisted—plain and simple food
Of all desirable variety—

And may not of ourselves seek to partake
That which would do us harm: Heaven is our friend.
Heaven's enemy will be our enemy,
And seek to bring us also into wo!

EVE. Heaven will, and thou wilt, be my guardian,
So dear to me, and chary of my good;
Therefore accept my humble gratitude.

ADAM. O, do not say, accept thy gratitude!
For rather I owe gratitude to thee,
Whose conversance hath been my great delight.
Heaven guard us!—Now yon trees I will attend
And do their pruning, while thou gatherest
Fruits for our morning meal, to which repast,
Upon this mossy rock, I will return,
When thou shalt call me hither to partake.

[*Exit* ADAM.

EVE. Thou mayst expect, then, to return ere long;
For soon the banquet will be all prepared.

Enter LUCIFER, *in shape of an Orang-outang.*[4]

LUC. [*Aside.*] She is alone, and opportunity
Now serves me: therefore let all wiles assist
In my designs; wiles from infernal depths,
Show me more false than is my shape assumed!
Fair woman [*approaching and addressing her*], and the fairest in this world,

Of all that's fair—ay, to the eye more pleasing
Than all else—I have been observing thee
Gathering with diligence these goodly fruits,
While native grace attends thy every move;
And on thy brow there is capacity
For all the knowledge that, in earth and heaven,
Awaits an infinite intelligence:
Though yet, methinks, thou hast not eaten of
The fruit possessing that mysterious power
To cause expansion intellectual,
Even to the wide range of infinity.

EVE. We eat of all the fruits that nourish us,
And what is hurtful that we must not eat.

LUC. There is a kind of fruit, of which, as yet,
Ye have not eaten, and which would perform
All I have said, and make ye what ye are not.

EVE. And what we would not wish to be, perhaps:
But where is there such fruit as thou speak'st of?

LUC. 'Tis here. [*Offers fruit of the forbidden tree.*

EVE. Oh! 'tis the fruit that would work death,
Which we have been commanded not to eat.

LUC. Yea, hath God said, ye shall not eat of all
The trees that yield mature their goodly fruits;
And this especially, the most ambrosial?

EVE. We may partake that which is wholesome food,
But that in th' midst this garden, God hath said,

"Ye shall not eat nor touch it, lest ye die;"
And what thou hast, is that pernicious fruit.
  Luc. O what an interdiction! what injustice!
How falsely represented is the fruit
That would make gods of ye! Ye shall not die;
For God doth know that in the very day
Ye eat thereof, ye shall perceive the truth,
And ye shall be as gods, knowing good and evil:
And more: by eating such continually,
Ye may, with aspirations infinite,
Advance to be the greatest gods in heaven!
I know thy nature craves ambrosial fruits,
That nourish earthly beings into gods;
And what thy godlike nature craves, is good
And wholesome; but from what it does not crave,
What need of strict command of abstinence?
  Eve. Dost thou eat of it? Thou art not a god;
For the deep earthly-seeming dullness of
Thy looks, belies thy specious reasoning.
Then eat the fruit thyself, and prove thy words:
If I could be a god by eating of it,
Thou couldst be something more than thou art now,
That stridest awkwardly thy shape uncouth
Along on devious way upon these flowers,
Which mars their beauty much.
  Luc. Fair woman,

My shape and manners, I am well aware,
Become not one who would be thy adviser;
Yet shapes uncouth, that dully stroll about
With awkwardness, may know a truth and tell it,
So that a fairer and more graceful one,
By giving heed, may gain advantages.
'Tis true, I have partaken of this fruit,
And by that means have made advancement great;
For hadst thou seen me ere I did partake,
My ugliest shape that sneaked among these shrubs,
Dreading the gaze of one fit for a god,
Would have surprised thy gazing with alarm:
Denied the power of speech—almost of thought—
I sought for food, and only dared be seen
By snakes, and toads, and meanest kinds of vermin,
That fled from me with fear at the first sight;
And while I digged for pig-nuts, I espied—
Turning my eyes whence came the balmy breeze,
Filled with voluptuous smell—this kind of fruit,
Of which I did partake immediately,
And am not as before, but what I am!
Wouldst thou have oculary evidence?
Behold, I taste again; see what I shall be!

[*He partakes of the fruit, and immediately assumes the appearance of an angel of light.*

Fair woman, wilt thou eat and be a god?

[*He presents her the fruit; she receives it*

EVE. O fruit ambrosial, that can change to gods
Those that partake; thy goodness I shall know,
And will, by thy mysterious power, be changed,
And be like to the greatest of the gods! [*Eats.*

LUC. Great be the change that fruit will work in ye!
Preparing of your banquet, never more
Avoid the fruit that will make gods of ye:
I must depart to where the gods abide. [*Exit.*

EVE. Is change so soon wrought in him by this fruit,
That he hath gone to where the gods abide?
Am I not now a god? O precious fruit!
Thy quality doth breed divinity
That doth inspire me. All this world is mine:
The sun is mine; so is the day it brings;
The moon is mine that smiles upon the night,
And all the stars are mine, and all these beasts,
Which now look fearful of me—all are mine!
By my persuasion, Adam shall partake
Of this fruit also and become a god;
And I will bring it to him now with haste. [*Exit.*

SCENE VI.

Ethereal Space.—*Enter* TWO ANGELS.

FIRST ANGEL.

Oh! man is fallen—fallen! it is done,
And evil flows destructive in his veins;
Even from this error are his ills begun,
And desolation in his being reigns,
Inviting anguish and afflictive pains,
Which he in his adversity must know;
And while in failing clay his spirit wanes,
The universal song hath ceased to flow,
And earth sends up a wail of everlasting wo.

SECOND ANGEL.

O Heaven! Oh, woful earth!—Oh, fallen man!
What darkness hangs upon his dreary way,
Who from the great creative edict sprang,
And has that edict dared to disobey,
And 'gainst Omnipotence, himself array,
In disregard of Heaven's—of nature's law;
Now all the universe feels dread dismay,

And shrinking back with sympathetic awe,
Sees Death and Hell gape wide to glut their ravenous
maw.

FIRST ANGEL.

Oh! dark and dreadful evil doth invade
The heart of man depraved by Heaven's Foe,
Who, from the fountain, hath insidious made
Destructive essence through life's currents flow,
That man might therefore naught of goodness know,
And his chained spirit sink beneath the care,
Of Hell's invidious might, usurping so,
That Death, through long eternity, might there,
Find immortality bewailing in despair!

SECOND ANGEL.

Yet Heaven is merciful as Heaven is just,
And will the fullness of that mercy share
On earth, among the creatures of the dust,
Formed in the image of th' Eternal there;
Though now despoiled the counterpart, so fair
When all his thoughts did flow in purity
Forth from the clear and happy fountain, where
Now dwells contamination, and a sea
Of desolation rolls on to eternity!

FIRST ANGEL.

Yea, goodness infinite will be revealed
'Twixt hell's dark regions and the realms of light;

And the deep wound on earth will yet be healed,
And all this foulest wrong give place to right,
By intercession of supernal Might,
Who will through sufferance the victory gain
O'er Death and Hell, that in eternal night
Shall dwell together, ever to remain
In all the agonies of everlasting pain! [*Exeunt.*

SCENE VII.

A Volcano.—Enter LUCIFER *and* BEELZEBUB.

BEEL. And the command that they should not partake
The fruit of such a tree, is disobeyed?
LUC. Well apprehended; and I will recount
Adventure there. The woman, whom I found
Alone, and gathering fruits for their repast
At morn, I did deceive with specious lies,
And such assurances as one would laugh
To think of—ay, that the forbidden fruit
Would not work death, but life, and they that eat
Thereof,. would be as gods.—Then she partook,
And quick began, with maudlin utterance,
To prate incessantly with phrase uncouth;

And I discovered, with observing care,
She, with the fruit destructive made fast way
To her companion, whom she quick beguiled
With hasty words smooth with persuasiveness,
And story of its power to change to gods,
All who partake of it: Then he partook,
And in his maudlin thought became a god:
Forthwith they fell to wrangling, and the beasts,
Affrighted, fled, or turned a scorning look,
Nor further would acknowledge him their lord.
There I continued lurking till the day
Began decline adown the sloping west,
At which time I did hear the judgment of
Offended Heaven, against offending man;
For Heaven, it proved, was conversant of all,
Since, that the universal Author's voice,
Unwelcome now in Eden, did pronounce
The judgment first on me as instigator —
That on the instigator shall recoil
Avenging punishment: Then let it come
Whenever it may come, if thus his threat,
He fain would think his power can execute.
Yet should it ever be, it would be joy
To know it is provoked by thwarting Heaven!
Next on the woman judgment was pronounced
In part: That she her progeny should bear

In sorrow, and that her desire should be
To her companion, and to him be subject.
Next, Adam listened to the consequence
In part to him, and thus it was pronounced;
"Because thou hast not hearkened unto me
But to thy wife, and eaten of the tree,
Of which I did command thee not to eat;
Therefore the ground is cursed for thy sake,
And thou henceforth shalt eat of it in sorrow,
And thorns and thistles it shall bear to thee,
And thou shalt eat of herbs, and in the sweat
Of thy face sunburnt get thy bread henceforth,
Until thy body shall return to dust;
For dust thou art and shalt to dust return."
Their woes are now begun—their being marred;
The circulating essence of their life,
Tainted with poison so their appetites,
Depraved, now crave the fruit which hastens death
Upon the body, while it mars the soul;
Each exercising mutual influence;
And through the law hereditary, shall
Man's progeny be tainted with this death,
From generation on to generation,
And so their aspirations shall be fixed
Low as the ground that bears their wayward tread.

BEEL. Ay, such will bring on earth confusion vast,

Which even is begun in paradise;
For looking from this mount, across that way
I surely saw such sights, and heard such sounds,
As would imply displeasure of the One
Who doth create, and doth regard his creatures.

LUC. Ay, thunders muttered in the darksome clouds
That gathered fast upon the burthenĕd air;
And lightnings broke anon, whence they, enchained,
Awaited edict, ere on wings of fire
They flew the fearful messengers of wrath
And the displeasure of creation's God.
Swift rushed the angry winds, and waters moved,
With murmurs dismal on their burthened waves;
Anon the beasts, already slunk away
From human gaze, began their farther haste
To forests dark, nor deigned a look behind;
So Heaven in anger frowned on paradise,
And angels from above on rapid wings,
Flew thither panoplied with swords of flame,
And shields of fire, and drove the human pair,
Now abject, forth from Eden desolate!
The orient way was held by cherubim,
And round the tree of life, a flaming sword
Turned every way to guard its wholesome fruit.

BEEL. May not the wrath of Heaven then serve our wiles,

And give consent vindictive to the woes,
That we inflict upon the creature man?

LUC. Heaven's anger may be kindled into flame,
To execute upon him punishment:
All this will follow from our diligence
Serving our enmity against th' Avenger,
Who will, no doubt, repent that he hath made
An image like himself, to be destroyed.

BEEL. Can we expect so much, nor fail in this?
It would repay us for our sufferings,
Since we did hasten out of heaven, repulsed,
With fury raging after us, and found
Such shelter only as th' abysm of wo
Afforded.

LUC. Yet can doubts possess thy thoughts,
That thou dost ask, "Can we expect so much,
Nor fail in this?" See what has now been done;
And on our bold emprises will success
Rise in triumphal and majestic state;
For much that will eventuate in time,
Awakes my prescience. Shall I show thee aught
Of great events that are in future yet?

BEEL. I would behold them. Canst thou show me them?

LUC. Ay, turn thy vision yonder. What seest thou
Through the discovered vista of hereafter,

Which brings to thy observance what shall be
Along Time's steady movement—what seest thou?
BEEL. I see a flood of waters pouring down
From blackest clouds; it spreads upon the earth,
A universal deluge, and drowning men
Cling fast to masses wrecked with thunderbolts,
O'er whom roll heavy surges; and far out,
A floating ark of huge bulk scorns the waves.
LUC. Thou seest the work of man's repenting Maker,
Who, fearful of our usurpation here,
Will fling destruction on his rebel creatures;
And, with vexed elements of earth and air,
Create confusion on th' external globe,
Infixing death on his marred images,
It grieves him so to look on, for he sees
Our triumph there, and his afflictive loss!
BEEL. Yet will he all destroy?
LUC. No: he will spare
A few, deemed good, to people earth again,
And think, no doubt, to end our domination:
The vainest thought! since all mankind will feel
Hereditary taint from th' fruit of evil,
And their curst appetites will crave it still.
BEEL. Great Lucifer, I clearly comprehend,
And I am ready to work vengeful spite,
By every means whatever it may be.

I see a flood of waters pouring down
From blackest clouds; it spreads upon the earth
A universal deluge.

PAGE 62.

LUC. I know thy power and will, and I chose well
When I appointed *thee* prince of the legions
I freed from Heaven's thralldom.—Now our way
Leads down into the chambers of the globe,
Where waiting myriads dominion hold
Over the elements they forge in shapes
Of missiles for all exigency made,
Should th' powers of heaven attempt here to dislodge us.
We go with counsels of our further work,
To our auxiliars vast in multitudes,
Sufficient for our multiplying need—
Whom we will make familiar with our cause,
And all man's attributes, that they may know
When to assail, and how; and they will do
The greater part the business we shall plan:
Yet that requiring greater power and skill,
Assign not to inferiority,
But will ourselves perform.—Wake hell in earth!

ECHO. *Wake hell in earth!*

BEEL. Whence did that echo come?
I think it came not from the concave sky.

LUC. It came not from the sky; the sky can not
Give out infernal echoes; but it pales
To hear the dreadful voice of Hell on earth,
Answered by myriads of the hosts of hell
Within it, whither now our way extends. [*Exeunt.*

SCENE VIII.

The Same.—Enter BEELZEBUB.

BEEL. Come forth, Diabolos and Mammon, come,
And Baccho; here attend immediately!

Enter DIABOLOS, MAMMON, *and* BACCHO.

DIAB. Great Prince, thy call has brought us quickly here:
What is there to be done at present time?
BEEL. Much: Cain and Abel, Adam's sons unlike,
Are now about to offer sacrifice
In yonder glade.—Go, interpose your powers
So Cain shall make a sacrifice of Abel.
DIAB. We will.
MAM. We will.
BAC. We will.
DIAB. We go at once,
And that shall be accomplished speedily!

[*Exeunt.*

SCENE IX.

A Glade, where there are two Altars.—Enter CAIN *and* ABEL.

ABEL. Here are the altars that I have prepared,
Which are awaiting now the sacrifice
That we will offer to indulgent Heaven;
And we will place our thoughts above the world,
And all things transitory.—Wait no more,
My brother Cain: wilt thou now sacrifice?

Enter DIABOLOS, MAMMON, *and* BACCHO, *invisible, with Wands.*—BACCHO *waves his Wand over* CAIN.

CAIN. If I delay, thou needst not: thou hast brought
The firstlings of thy flock, and thou mayst first
Begin thy offering; for I shall first
Offer this liquor to my fervent thirst.

ABEL. O Cain, refrain! It is the noxious fruit
That worketh death!

CAIN. What if it worketh death?

I have partaken oft, and will again. [*Drinks.*

[MAMMON *waves his Wand over* CAIN.

What need have I to offer sacrifice
On a consuming altar?—will it profit?

ABEL. O Cain, my brother! I will offer now
My sacrifice to God, and in my prayer
I will remember thee.

CAIN. Then offer now
Thy sacrifice, and pray too, if thou wilt,
But not for me; for I can sacrifice,
And do my praying too, when I desire.

ABEL. O Cain! beware lest God be angry with thee,
And not accept thy sacrifice when offered.

CAIN. Presumer, what hast thou to do with that?
Offer thy sacrifice, and I will mine;
And see which will be more acceptable.

ABEL. By faith, I know my sacrifice will be
Accepted, though I am unworthy of it.

[*They build fires upon their altars, and place upon them their offerings.*

CAIN. The slow fire dies beneath my offering,
While to the clouds the flame of thine ascends.
Is not my offering as good as thine?
Why, then, is thine accepted, and not mine?
Well, I will offer now good sacrifice
To Heaven, by making sacrifice of thee!

[CAIN *beats* ABEL *with a club.*

ABEL. What dost thou now, my brother? O my brother!
Thou knowest not thy deed, and I forgive thee:
May Heaven forgive thee also, O my brother!

[ABEL *dies.*—*Exeunt* MAMMON *and* BACCHO.

DIAB. Ha! it is well performed. I will remember
His offering—a human sacrifice:
There shall be many such upon this world!

[*Exit* DIABOLOS.

CAIN. What have I done? Is this my brother Abel?
And am I Cain? Oh! now my soul awakes
To the severe reality of this!—
Yet why may I not possibly mistake?
Arise, my brother Abel! Art thou dead,
That thou dost lie so still?—for thy pale cheek
Doth wear a smile upon it! Art thou dead?
And Cain thy murderer? It was not Cain;
For he is saddest mourner of thy death;
But 'twas the evil spirit that inhabits
The frequent potions of my thirst depraved,
That holds my soul in thralldom absolute,
And doth beget within me hellish deeds!
My younger brother Abel—O my brother!
Thou, guardian angel, didst admonish me;
And if I had obeyed thy admonitions,

I had not now occasion to repent
Of such a deed as this, for which, I fear,
Vengeance will overtake me. Why these fears?
Are they the harbingers of punishment,
Or but creations of a guilty conscience?

Re-enter DIABOLOS, *and waves his Wand over* CAIN.

No matter which. The deed is done.—Away,
Ye tell-tale fears, that would expose my crimes,
With guilty habitation on my features!
With stern denial I will dare to meet
The powers vindictive both in earth and heaven!

[*A Voice from above is heard.*

VOICE. Cain! Cain! where is thy brother?

CAIN. I know not:
Am I my brother's keeper?

VOICE. What hast thou done?
Thy brother's blood hath now a voice that crieth
To me from th' ground, and tells thy guilty deed,
For which thou now art cursed from the earth,
Which, at thy hand, received thy brother's blood.
When thou dost till the ground, it shall not yield
Henceforth to thee her strength: a fugitive
And vagabond shalt thou be in the earth!

[*Exit* DIABOLOS.

CAIN. My punishment is more than I can bear;

For thou this day hast driven me from out
The face of earth, and from thy face shall I
Be hid; and I shall be a fugitive
And vagabond in th' earth; and it shall be
That every one that findeth me, shall slay me!
VOICE. Fear not; for whosoever slayeth Cain,
On him shall seven-fold vengeance be imposed.
CAIN. A mark is set upon me: therefore, man,
I know, shall not be instrument of vengeance;
For none shall kill me.—I must go away:
My power is failing, and I must not stay! [*Exit.*

SCENE X.

A Volcano.—Enter LUCIFER *and* BEELZEBUB.

BEEL. The flood is past, the great flood Heaven did send
To drown the world of our supremacy,
Yet sent in vain, as coming time must prove.
The waters are subsided, and our spies,
Most vigilant, make swiftly here and hence,
Their coming and their going, on dark wings
Through the pale ether.
LUC. It is even thus:

BEEL. One thousand and six hundred years ago,
Two score and seventeen in the addition—
Thou didst unveil the future to my view,
And I beheld the earth drowned with this flood
Which has not long been off the humid earth.
LUC. Wouldst thou behold the future yet again,
That thou dost speak of this?
BEEL. I would.
LUC. Behold!
With thy expectant vision turned across
The way of Ararat into the blue,
That draws aside, discovering to thy view,
The proof of what our diligence shall do:—
What there so interests thy wondering gaze?
BEEL. Upon a mountain, just outside a city,
I see a cross whereon a being like
The Son of God, bows low his pallid brow:
Now darkness hides the sun; the earth quakes,
And rocks are rent asunder there, and graves
Yawn tenantless of their awakened dead:
Now round the cross, the multitude, as though
Disquieted with fears, go to and fro,
Pale as the sea when startled winds disturb
To an awakening fright its slumbering breast;
Even as when we, upon our journey here,
Turned our swift course across the watery realm,

That felt the very shadow of our flight,
While fear impressed the air, that fled in tempests
Along the frightened main!

Luc. All that thou seest
Will come to pass: That was the Son of God,
Who terminated the celestial war—
In which we were almost victorious,
When from the concave of his lifted shield,
Then made offensive armor fronting us,
Shot volleys of transcendent light across
Our ranks unable to withstand its glare
All sudden and unwonted—and pursued
Our flying legions then, with fiery tempests,
That *sighing to his armory returned*,
When we had passed beyond heaven's opened walls!
Yet time will give us opportunity
To wreak on him accumulated hate;
And though he knows our purpose thwarted once,
He yet shall know he can not thwart revenge:
Even though victory at last should be
On the Almighty's side, and we be driven
Again to feel no respite of our pain
By vexing the inhabitants of earth,
Yet, if the most his subjects be our captives,
To writhe forever in consuming wrath,
How dear to him will be that victory!

For this cause, yet Heaven's own begotten Son
Shall suffer the severest suffering:
As we unwilling anguish must endure,
And feel the wrath of the Eternal One,
So, He shall feel the burthen of our hate:
O sweet revenge! that makes a heaven of hell!

BEEL. O sweet revenge! that makes a heaven of hell!

LUC. Again the habitants of earth are few,
And all our forces need not be in action
Until occasion shall require. I now go down
Among them and their revelings, and when
The time is fit, Diabolos will come
To do thee offices on Ararat,
All which have been delivered to thy charge. [*Exit.*

BEEL. And which are being performed: And now I see
By observation in the orient,
Typhon in haste, and on his way attends
Silence and shades, while evening comes apace;
And the hushed air broods with a mournful quiet
Along the waste of death.

Enter TYPHON.

TYPH. All hail! great Prince.

BEEL. What favor more? Doth opportunity
Wait on advancing time and on our wiles?

TYPH. I bring more tidings ; thou canst better judge
What opportunities they may unfold.

BEEL. I think before they are delivered, I
Well apprehend what thy report will show:
Is th' vineyard fully grown which has been planted
By Lamach's son, who, with his family,
Came from the ark to people earth again ?
And is its fruit mature, and juice expressed,
Yet stale and noxious, so that we may have[5]
No more delay in tempering again,
To suit our purposes, to deeper taint,
The members of this family of Noah,
Which has been saved from the prevailing flood ?

TYPH. The lusty vineyard yields its fruit mature,
And nocent preparation of its juice
Fermented, has been well attended to.
When will we have the revelings which thou
Didst promise ? for my service has been much,
And well performed.

BEEL. It has, I am assured ;
Recount it : all thy deeds shall have reward.

TYPH. Why, I did course along the troubled spume
Of the deep waters, following the ark
On devious way, with fluctuating winds,

Day after day, night after night, even while
The elements were leagued against me so,
My way was difficult along the flood;
And some celestial spirit, as I told thee
A time before, did strive to thwart my course,
Amalgamating air and fire and noise,
With which my way was vexed with usage rough;
And when the ark did rest on Ararat,
Which I did haste to bring thee tidings of,
Then that celestial spirit interposed,
And raised a tempest all of fire across
My flight, which took me from my course awry
More than a thousand leagues, whence I did toil
Against the speed of flame, back on my way.

BEEL. Well, Typhon, brave Typhon, thou didst well.
Thy service there was much, though not to me
More than thyself; the gain is shared alike,
That comes by any of our separate acts
In common cause.

TYPH. I have done other things;
I have been vigilant on Ararat
Where rests the great ark empty of all life;
Thence swift to thee, oft tidings I did bring—
Of Noah going with his family,
And every animal; all flesh, both fowl

And cattle; even every creeping thing,
Out of the ark; and of the sacrifice—
Which, on an altar, he did make to Heaven—
Of one of every cleanly beast and fowl,
Burnt to a smelling savor as offensive
To me, as any could be sweet to Heaven.

BEEL. All that was well which thou didst; all was well:
Thou art a brave spirit who, bravest deeds,
Art able to perform: Thou didst else there.

TYPH. Yes, other things I did on Ararat;
Beneath the rainbow of God's covenant,
I heard the oracle he did pronounce—
That not again for man's sake would he curse
The ground, for the imagination of
Man's heart is evil, even from his youth—
Nor yet again smite any living thing;
And while the earth remains, seed time and harvest
And cold, and heat, and summer and winter,
And day, and night, should cease not: this I heard
And brought the tidings of it.

BEEL. Very well,
Brave Typhon, well: we shall have revelings
Ere long, yet something else is to be done,
On Ararat, with essence very vile,
So that man's heart being evil from his youth,

Shall yet become most evil from his youth,
By an enlarged inheritance of ill,
From much addition to the taint which flows
Pernicious through the fountain of his life.
The time is fit; Come forth, Diabolos,
And Imp, and Baccho, come!

Enter DIABOLOS, IMP, *and* BACCHO.

DIAB. Hail! here we are,
And at your service.
BEEL. There is business now;
The vineyard is mature on Ararat;
There do your offices: Intoxication
Shall revel on the mountain, and the spirit
Of man be tempered to our very wish;
And progeny succeeding progeny,
Shall long experience the sure effects.
DIAB. I will attend the full accomplishment.
O, I could blow a breath and split the sea,
And it would fear for ever to unite
Again its severed waters, holding back
Against attractive forces all their bulk!
O I could pluck the moon out of its orbit,
So we could walk the night in thicker darkness,
Without that glaring eye upon our way!
But such doth not behoove us now to do. [*Exeunt.*

SCENE XI.

ARARAT.—*Enter* NOAH, *from a tent.* DIABOLOS, TYPHON, IMP, *and* BACCHO, *at a distance, departing.*

NOAH. O why by daytime came such heavy night
Upon my spirit, that it sank in sleep,
From which forgetfulness, I have awaked?
My senses have been drowned in poisonous draught,
To which partaking, I had been deceived
By Ham, my son, who will not heed advice,
But to indulgence yields his appetite,
That injuries upon his soul and body,
Course through his veins.

Enter SHEM, HAM, *and* JAPHETH!

O Ham, my son!
What is it thou hast done to me?

HAM. Nothing,
But the good wine this vineyard doth produce,
I gave to thee, and of thy own accord
Thou didst partake; naught further have I done.

NOAH. Thou art my son, and disputation now,

Need not encroach upon this interview,
But condemnation falls upon thy acts;
For by thy wickedness thou hast provoked
Heaven's judgment which is given me to pronounce
On Canaan—name of thy posterity.
Cursed be Canaan; a servant, he
Of servants, shall unto his brethren be.[6]
But blessed be the Lord, the God of Shem,
And Canaan to him shall render service.
God shall enlarge Japheth, and he shall dwell
In th' tents of Shem, and Canaan shall serve him.

[*Exeunt.*

SCENE XII.

A Volcano.—Enter BEELZEBUB, *meeting* DIABOLOS, TYPHON, IMP, *and* BACCHO.

BEEL. Infernal spirits, is your charge performed?
DIAB. It is, and we left Noah in his tent
And overcome with the stale juice of grape,
So that he knew not that he was alive;
And Ham has been our instrument in this,
Who had been plied with vileness potable;
And his regard paternal is destroyed

By his oft bibings; and the crimson life
Is tainted with the essences of ill.

BEEL, Ha! Thence will follow acts which we shall urge —
Bickerings, jealousies, hate, strife, stratagems,
Spoils, murders, and revenge: all these shall be
Even as before the flood.

DIAB. I have no doubt
That all the world would yet again be drowned,
Because of our successful policies,
If Heaven had not decreed it otherwise.

BEEL. What if, with fire it shall be burned to ashes,
And be resolved to ether, and be drawn
To other spheres, by gravitating force,
And gathered into their circumference?

DIAB. Where then would be the spirits that we torment?
Would their essential beings be consumed;
And so the acts that we delight in, end?

BEEL. No: Spirits of the earth that then be damned,
Will suffer wrath that burns continual,
Which the material fires within this world
Scarce counterfeit with all their violence.
Those torments are within us endless fixed,
Where'er we be, nor aught can multiply,
Nor aught decrease, save the delight we feel

For having caused mankind to share them too.
According to appointment, now the time
Is fit to revel in the fiery deep.
Come now, ye spirits, who have lately served
My will on Ararat, effectual,
And revel in the furnace of the world!

DIAB. Through the hiatus large, spout liquid fires,
And blow fierce flames; that will be revelry.

TYPH. 'T was promised us to revel, so we will,
In manner suitable, and that, to me,
Will be to forge the elemental fire,
To lightnings, and, astride them, course the deep.

IMP. And manner suitable to me will be
To grasp the lightnings and entangle them
In strife for separation, and so forth.

[*Exeunt all but* BACCHO.

BAC. The meaning of that *so forth* must be drinking; for there be no real revelry that drinking be not companion of; and for such I am well prepared with the good spiritual essence in this crucible; and which doth elevate the spirit to the full enjoyment of revelry. It is this that I do mingle in the stale grape-juice for mankind, and thereby they fall into revelries, and fightings, and many other good mischiefs — all which follow *so forth* if *so forth* be really drinking. [*Exit.*

SCENE XIII.

A Forest in JUDEA.—*Enter* LUCIFER *and* BEELZEBUB.

LUC. Dost thou think so? well, do thy will in this.
BEEL. I see the doubt that weighs upon thy answer,
Can we not then destroy his incarnation,
While yet in infancy?
LUC. Whether or not,
Make trial: send Diabolos, who shall
Destroy all the first born in Bethlehem
And the surrounding regions.
BEEL. We will then
Make sure of the Redeemer and the kingdom,
Which may be without end, though we shall reign.

Enter TYPHON.

Why, Typhon, dost thou tremble in thy haste?
Why dost thou put such agitation on?
TYPH. Did ye not see the light: Did ye not hear
The noise tremendous, like a trumpet sounding
Loud in the sky, with strange and awful meaning.

BEEL. We did, and know its import: Dost thou know
Where is Diabolos?

TYPH. Near Bethlehem,
Attending to the murder of some footmen.

BEEL. Not now, I see; for hither on his way
Diabolos doth shade the eye of night.

Enter DIABOLOS.

DIAB. Hail, Lucifer! Beelzebub — all hail!
There now is cause for great activity.

BEEL. There ever is much cause for us to act:
What special cause invests thee now with dread
Or seeming fear, who art so wonted brave?

DIAB. Did ye not see the light nor hear the voice
More dreadful than the thunders of the deep?
Oh, it hath frightened me more than the terrors
That followed us precipitant from heaven!

BEEL. We saw the light and heard pronunciation
Fall from the sky, much heavier than thunders;
But what of that — can light or noise affright thee?

DIAB. O Lucifer, when I did venture forth,
In lunar light, to tread the way of death,
And aid some night-assassins seeking blood,
A blazing star, on sudden, lit the skies,
And slow descending, eastward moved until,
O'er Bethlehem it stood and cast a gleam

Of vivid light athwart the way of night.
Anon a voice from heaven did shake the earth;
And thus it fell with all its terrors down:
"Now unto us a child is born; to us
A Son is given; the government shall be
Upon his shoulders, and his name be called
Wonderful, Counselor, the Mighty God,
The everlasting Father, th' Prince of Peace."
Will not our warfare soon be brought to close?
For He of whom the ancient prophets spoke
Is come t' assume the guardianship of men.
Fear fills me now, which anger might dispel,
If I, with wrath, could fright the powers of Heaven,
Nor think of accident upon my way.

BEEL. Fear not while thou art willing to perform
A deed the stars will pale to look upon;
For thou wouldst intercept, as well as we,
Encroachment on this government of ours;
Therefore, ere thou didst come, we had determined,
That thou shouldst do more acts in Bethlehem,
According with thy honorable name,
So worthy hitherto from worthy deeds.

DIAB. I have done very much upon the earth;
And will do all that may advance our rule.

BEEL. Art thou prepared to do what we propose
If it should be to slay the dread Messiah?

DIAB. Ay, that I will, if it be in my power.
BEEL. 'T is that we had determined.
DIAB. Who shall be
The instrument in this: It shall be done.
BEEL. Herod the king, who, jealous of his throne,
Shall fear Messiah here will reign instead.
Go, trouble him with this till he shall seek
Messiah's life while yet he is an infant:
Go, ply thy effort well.
DIAB. That will I do;
For I did make him slay his sons and wife,
And I will make him take Messiah's life. [*Exeunt.*

SCENE XIV.

A Room in HEROD'S *Palace.—Enter* HEROD, *and* Valet *bearing Wine, of which* HEROD *partakes.*

HER. Go to my officers without delay,
And tell them I desire their presence here.
[*Exit* Valet.
The wise men whom I sent to Bethlehem
Have mocked me; for they deign not to return,
And bring me word if they have found the child
By diligence of search, as I commanded:

And it is possible my feigned design
To worship him may be suspected false,
That they have not returned to me again.
Yet 'tis determined that he shall be slain,
Though Bethlehem and all the coasts thereof
Be deluged with a billowy flood of tears:—
Even though the voice of weeping lamentation
Should crack the sky, and trouble all the air
So it would whisper sorrows o'er the world!

Enter Officers.

1ST OFF. Thy royalty looks pale: art thou not well?
HER. I am quite well, although Jerusalem,
Yea, all Judea, hath a sickness on her
Which naught except chirurgery can cure;
And ye are the physicians I have chosen.
1ST OFF. Why, we are not physicians, nor know we
Of any sickness come upon the kingdom—
Which, if we were to know, should we attempt
The office of a surgeon, such beginning
Might be most dangerous empiricism.
3D OFF. I am prepared to do thy utmost will,
Though it should be to probe Jerusalem,
Or amputate the limb of Bethlehem,
Or any other that may pain the kingdom.
HER. I am the heart which in this kingdom beats,

To whom, and from whom, flow the currents of life;
And from its sickness I am languishing:
Therefore it is ye see that I am pale.
A vein in Bethlehem must now be lanced;
Then will the life essential to my life
Flow healthily as wont.—Now go ye forth:
In Bethlehem, and all the coasts thereof,
Slay every male child two years old and under!

1ST OFF. [*Aside to the* Officers.] Is he not mad?

2D OFF. There is another fit of slaughter on him.

3D OFF. We must obey, or be ourselves his victims;
Yet conscience smites me when I smite to death.

1ST OFF. Soft, I will speak with him, that we may know
If his sincerity demands this deed.—
Great King, obedience to your royalty;
But may I ask, what ails your kingdom, that
Such slaughter only can recover it,
That th' air would all be pierced with shrieks of grief?

HER. None but physicians this can understand;
And thou art no physician, so thou saidst:
Wherefore should explanations waste my breath?
It is decreed: therefore it shall be done!

1ST OFF. Oh, sickening remedy! the kingdom must
Drink the magnetic life of infant blood;
To heal the kingdom thus, will make me sick.

HER. Art thou a man? What is thy liver made of,
That thou dost even pale to think of blood?
Drink thou of this. Nay, start not; 'tis not blood!
Drink: it will give thee spirit of a man—
Drink, all of ye, this fear-dispelling drink!

[HEROD *drinks, then the* Officers *drink, of the wine.*

Can ye not murder now? can ye not slay
The young in Bethlehem?

3D OFF. I have killed men:
But—to kill a child—

HER. Drink more of this:
Drink, all of ye! [HEROD *and* Officers *drink.*
Can ye not kill a child?

1ST OFF. Yes, I can kill more than a hundred children,
By cutting off their heads!

2D OFF. Ho! I can kill
More than a thousand, dashing out their brains!

3D OFF. And if their mothers make noise by crying, it will be real music, nor will we relent.—Let us go. Blood! blood!—infants' blood! It will please our King, whose officers we are; and we are loyal!

[*Exeunt.*

SCENE XV.

A Wilderness in JUDEA. — *Enter* LUCIFER, BEELZEBUB, DIABOLOS, MAMMON, TYPHON, IMP, *and* BACCHO.

LUC. From thy first intimation, I did doubt
That in his infancy we could prevail
Against the Son incarnate on the earth.

BEEL. But how did he escape? The star appeared
O'er Bethlehem, and every male child there,
Under two years, was slain.

LUC. Heaven's ministers,
That hither oft come from the empyrean
On errands from the Throne, must have forewarned
His parents, that they fled with him beyond
The region that was doomed to infant slaughter;
And, from neglected watch, he did escape
The fate thou didst assign his infancy
In that design, and though in its attempt
So unsuccessful, worthy yet no less.

BEEL. Those white-winged messengers have oftentimes

From their celestial habitation come,
With hinderance upon our efforts here,
And great vexation. Must we suffer it?
Shall we not rather wage against them war,
And hurl upon their way hell's missive fire,
To turn them quickly back in thither haste
Where they may find immured security?
Luc. Nay, verily; for they will not perform
Much that we may not turn to our account,
If we have care upon man's appetite.
Diab. Ay, through abnormal appetite indulged,
Our power upon the world is very great.
We fain would have all feasting here abound,
But never fasting, since thereby mankind
Become less subject to our influence:[7]
For verily, for forty days and nights
Did Moses fast; and then, despite my power,
He held with the Jehovah audience
Upon Mount Sinai, and from him received
Two tablets with the written decalogue.
Typh. And when Elijah fasted in the desert,
I could not exercise him with my power.
Luc. And now, in the Judean desert, Christ
Is fasting; and I think the time has come,
That, with temptation, I may break that fast—
Which, to accomplish, thither I will go,

And make experiment with deepest wiles.
What if I overcome him, and traduce
Him from the side of Heaven? No virtue then
Could turn against us the Redeemer's power!
But if that fast I break not with the craving
Of long-unsatiated appetite,
Then shall my effort be to gain accord
Of act to my desire, thereby to gain
Upon him influence, and open thus
Insidious way for my advancing wiles;
Or, failing still, advantage I will take
Of the chief object of his mission here,
Which is, to bear the weight of man's transgression,
And guide his footsteps from the ways of death,
Wherein my influence leads him to walk:
Therefore will I make specious promises,
That, if he worship me, I will resign
My power on earth, that he may have all sway;
And I no more will tempt mankind astray;
And then he need not die upon the cross,
And groan beneath the weight of agonies:
And should I gain compliance happily,
Since he is here exemplar for mankind,
Then all mankind will bow and worship me:
Such be attempt! If no success attend,
Then through the influence of essence vile,

We yet will have all things to our desire;
For by experiments we shall enhance
The potency of all polluting draughts.—
I go; and ye will respite here awhile,
Reflecting on successes of the past,
While thither to Messiah now I haste. [*Exit* LUCIFER.

BEEL. Let all success await thy great attempt!

BAC. I rather judge that I, with food or drink
Of good-vile quality, might overcome
Messiah's fasting: there is mighty power
In wines made goodly vile by mixing in
Decoction of strong roots digged secretly.

BAC. I have done very much in times now past.

BEEL. Thou hast, for which thou art deserving much.

IMP. Much service I have done upon the world,
Going on errands in the open day,
Exposed to light, and also in the night!
And swiftly through the elemental air,
When lightnings pierced it, and the furious storms
Threatened the stationed forests, went my way.

MAM. And much have I done also, purchasing
Man's quintessential life with little gold—
Making him lie for but a little gold;
Making him steal for but a little gold;
Making him kill for but a little gold!

DIAB. Ay, thou didst much when I assisted thee,

Conjuring conscience quite inaudible,
And in man's heart inspiring influence.
BAC. O that was easy after I had made
Them drink the juices stale of grape and palm—
Then thou couldst easily inspire them, for
Their consciences went out when drink went in.
I have done very many other things—
With swine-fat I have vexed the crimson life,
Especially upon the sultry days,
Producing counterfeit of maudlin wrath;
Thence followed jealousies and bickerings,
And envy, strife, and animosities:
O should I tell the half my deeds besides,
The tale would lengthen till the end of time!
IMP. 'T is said that at the end of time this world
Is to be burned as Nineveh was burned.
Thinking of Nineveh, I think again
Of very many great achievements.
BAC. Then
Thou thinkst of *my* achievements, for they be
So very many and so very great.
IMP. I think of very many errands which
I did in Nineveh, when Gabriel
And other angels often crossed my way;
But I avoided them and did all things
According to direction:——

BAC. And the inhabitants of Nineveh,
And Sodom, and Gomorrah,—which with fire
From heaven were burned,—were of the race of Ham
Whom I did goodly-vilely qualify;
Therefore, contamination and a thirst
For nocent draughts, was their inheritance.

TYPH. Think ye what I did on the plains of Shinar,
When men were snoring discords on the night;—

IMP. If there be any discords in thy tale,
Let it be long and not have any end.

TYPH. O do not break it into pieces then.

IMP. Say on, and I will neither speak nor snore,
Lest such a kind of melody expand
My nostril, that thou wouldst be quickly seized
With very rapture, and at once forget
That thou art not above in heaven!

TYPH. In th' plains of Shinar, when the sun had led
The day behind the occidental steep,
In huddled tents, forgetfulness reposed
With men, and snoring vexed the sleepy night;
Then went I careful forth, and in their ears
Whispered the greatness of enduring name;
And in their minds inspired essential pride,
And fear that time would blot their memory:
So when the morning called them, hastily
Up they arose and rubbed their sleepy eyes,

And, running to and fro, cried with loud voice,
" Ho! Let us build a city and a tower
Whose top shall reach the heavens, and make ourselves
A name, lest we be scattered o'er the earth,
And its broad shores receive our wandering tribes."
With brick and mortar, they began to build
A city and a tower, whose altitude
Should reach the heavens, to make themselves a name,
Lest they should be divided, and abroad
Be scattered on the face of all the earth.
Then was the King of heaven provoked to wrath
Who, in his anger, scattered far and wide,
With their changed dialects the tribes of men.
BAC. O, that was Babel! and the founders of
All that confusion, were one Nimrod and
One Asshur, who were also lineal
In th' race of Ham, who was contaminate
From the best good-vile liquor that I gave him:
And they were very mighty rebels too;
For Nimrod hunted men—made them depart
From th' teachings far, of Shem's posterity.[9]
I made the Shechemites so merry too,
With goodly drink, that they conspired against
Abimelech. I made the Ephraimites
Drunkards, and the kings sick with drunkenness;

And, with the very good-vile liquor, I
Did even turn the prophets out their way;
I made them err in vision and in judgment
Stumble. In Babylon, besides, I brought
Riot and vomiting and filthiness:
I made the nations drunken with her wine,
So madness and destruction did abound.

DIAB. Madness, murder, havoc, war, revenge,
I have excited over all the earth,
And hell rejoiceth therefore.

BEEL. Worthy, all,
Because your deeds have vexed the world so much
That we behold its many miseries.
The tide of life wells from the heart of man,
Mingled with entity malign, which shapes
Excrescences of mental counterparts
That give expression to our influence,
Which works upon the earth's inhabitants,
Destruction.—Let us depart apace;
For, through the sky, illumination glows
Empyreal along the coming way
Of angels hitherward, and it behooves
Not now that we surprise them with alarm. [*Exeunt.*

Enter several ANGELS.

1ST ANG. Not to the Tempter, favor in regard

Will the Messiah yield although the wiles
Of Lucifer should seem to show awhile
The speciousness of fair expedience
To be compliance with infernal will.

2D ANG. No ; the Messiah, who is now incarnate
Because of sin upon the world, hath come
In order to redeem mankind from death ;
Nor will he yield to aught Hell may propose,
And so will Heaven be glorified in him ;
And, faithful to our charge when Lucifer
Shall flee from him confounded with defeat,
To him will we proceed and minister.
Meanwhile we go to the Judean desert,
And there keep distant watch; while Christ is led
Forth by the tempter, him will we observe
Where'er he may depart. [*Exeunt.*

SCENE XVI.

Wilderness in JUDEA.—*Enter* CHRIST *and* LUCIFER *meeting.*

LUC. Hail, whosoe'er thou art! Behold I not
One who is more than man? Art thou not He
Of whom the prophets spake—the Son of God,
Who, it is said, would miracles perform?
Command thou then that these stones be made bread;
And if thy mandate cause them thus to change,
Thou shalt have proof that thou art even He,
And thou mayst eat thy fill, for I perceive
That thou art hungered.——

CHRIST. I know thee, who thou art—the Evil One.
And dost thou think I know not who *I* am?
Besides, 't is written that man shall not live
By bread alone, but he shall nourishment
Receive from every word that cometh from
The mouth of God.

LUC. 'T is truly written thus.
Let us go forth into Jerusalem;

For I would learn of thee, that I may there
Find opportunity for veriest proof
That thou art the Messiah—Prince of Peace!
For I am willing to make compromise,
Which may result with favor to his mission.
  CHRIST. I will go there into the holy city,
But will not yield obedience to thee,
Although my sufferance admits thy presence. [*Exeunt.*

SCENE XVII.

CHRIST *and* LUCIFER *on a Pinnacle of the Temple in* JERUSALEM.

  LUC. I fain would know if thou art the Messiah:
If thou be He, cast thyself down; for it
Is written, "He shall give his angels charge
Concerning thee, and in their hands shall bear
Thee up, lest thou, at any time, shouldst dash
Thy foot against a stone."
  CHRIST. 'T is said, "Thou shalt not tempt the Lord
    thy God."
  LUC. Is it temptation then, to seek to know,
Of certainty, who is the Son of God
That, on conditions, I may favor show,

By yielding to his everlasting sway?
Yet thou didst intimate in thy reply,
That thou art He. I will presume thou art,
Since thou didst know me on my first approach:
Even as thou saidst, I am the Evil One.
And none I think on earth, save the Messiah,
In my dissimulation, could perceive
That verily I am the enemy
That long 'gainst Heaven have striven, not in vain,
Which thou and all celestial powers well know.
From yonder mountain of exceeding height—
That overlooks the kingdoms of the world,
Which I have oft surveyed in my regard—
We may behold their partial magnitude.
Thither let us repair if thou wouldst know
What I am willing to resign to thee;
And the conditions I will there make known.

CHRIST. I will go to the summit of the mountain,
And view the kingdoms which I must redeem;
And though thy presence may accompany,
By my permission now, that thou mayst see
How great thy ultimate discomfiture;
Thou needst not think to move me from my mission:
Thy power is finite and thou canst not move
The Rock which is the world's sole, safe foundation.

[*Exeunt.*

SCENE XVIII.

CHRIST *and* LUCIFER *on the Summit of a high Mountain — Cities in the distance.*

LUC. Look thou upon the extended country round —
Into the east, and west, and north, and south:
Whichever way thou turnest, kingdoms vast,
With their great cities spotting here and there
The hills and plains far as the eye extends,
Fill with their glory the surrounding view.
I reign triumphant over all of these:
My will is the great impulse of the world;
For in the coursing essence of man's life —
In all the currents leading to the soul,
I have enhanced hereditary ill
By ministrations of the evil fruit;
And Nature's efforts can not overcome
The working mischief, nor is heavenly grace
Sufficiency to change all human hearts,
Till I resign all willingly to thee,
And strive no more against the powers of heaven.
Then think again upon thy mission here:

Look thou upon the extended country round—
Into the east and west, and north and south.

PAGE 100.

Canst thou relieve the world of all its ill
Unless I cease my efforts to increase it,
Withdrawing all my power to give thee sway?
It will not be an easy thing to bear
The weight of man's transgression: this would press
The crimson life-drops through thy very pores;
And ere the cup be drank even to its dregs
The language of thy deepest groan would be
A prayer to be relieved, if possible,
From deepest anguish of thy burthened spirit!
And would such prayer be heard? No; not in heaven,
Nor even in hell save it be uttered now!
Yet 'tis not meet that thou shouldst suffer thus —
No; grant me one request; and all the sway
I hold upon the earth, I will resign,
And never more go forth to tempt mankind;
And thy devoted subject man shall be.
Now if thou wouldst all men should honor thee,
Do this one thing — fall down and worship me.[10]

CHRIST. Hence — get thee, Satan: it is written thou
Shalt worship God — Him only shalt thou serve.

[*Exit* SATAN, *and immediately several* Angels *enter, and with the Messiah depart.*

SCENE XIX.

CALVARY.—JESUS, *with a crown of thorns on his head, on a Cross, between two* Malefactors. *A Multitude*—Officers, Soldiers, *and* Citizens—*about them. Above* JESUS, *on the Cross, in letters of Greek, Latin, and Hebrew, is written the superscription of his accusation*—"THIS IS JESUS, THE KING OF THE JEWS."

CHRIST. Father,
Forgive them; for they know not what they do!
OFF. Since he saved others, let him save himself,
If he be Christ—the chosen One of God.
SOLD. If, as thou saidst, thou be King of the Jews,
Now save thyself, and then we will believe.
1ST MAL. If thou be Christ, then save thyself and us.
2D MAL. O, dost not thou fear God, seeing thou art
In the same condemnation?—we indeed
Justly, for we receive the due reward
For that which we have done; but this man hath
Done naught amiss.—My Lord, remember me
When thou dost come into thy kimdom!——

CHRIST. To-day shalt thou, with me in paradise,
Find happiness immortal!——
Eloi! Eloi! lama sabachthani?
[*A* Soldier *offers him vinegar in a sponge on a reed.*[11]

OFF. He calleth for Elias. Let us see
If from the dead, to save him, he will come.

CHRIST. Father, into thy hands I now commend
My spirit.—IT IS FINISHED! [*Dies.*

'Twas then the temple's vail was rent in twain;
The sun shrunk with amazement from the sight,
And graves yawned tenantless; and as the main
Is oft by startled winds awaked to fright
And sudden paleness, so did fear alight
Upon the multitude which, to and fro,
Trod apprehensive through the dreadful night
That till the ninth hour palled the very glow
Of the diurnal course, and frightened Hellbelow!

END OF PART I.

I comply with your request for I am not only willing but desire to deliver in this form what I believe to be the true meaning of the scriptural language expressing the primal Curse.

I am Your Obt Servt
Jerome Kidder

PART SECOND.

SCENE I.

A Country in SPAIN.—*Enter* BEELZEBUB *and* DIABOLOS.

DIAB. Why should the voyage be prevented? why
Not rather hasten it? We have discovered
Such potency in this distilled liquid,
I think we ought to fill the earth with it—
Even all the western continent, where now
The red man of the savage wilderness
Wars on opposing tribes: give this to them,
And havoc will increase.

BEEL. Great Lucifer
Hath said, "Beware!—let no ship sail that way."
His wisdom doth direct, nor know I yet
In full why it may be of service that
We thwart all expedition to the West.

Enter TYPHON.

Hast thou performed thy charge at Salamanca?

TYPH. Ay, to the full; and if thou hadst been there,
Thou wouldst have laughed.
BEEL. Why dost thou think I would?
TYPH. To hear the language of a hundred mouths,
That gave out, in as many different tones,
Objection to discourage all adventure
Across the billowy and frothy sea.
Thus from one organ issued gravest speech:—
"It can not be; for such opinion is
At variance with all geography
Of earth and sky, as taught in holy scripture."
Another—"O preposterous presumption,
And big absurdity!—I will not listen,
My ears do pain me so." Another said,
With grave accordance on his emphasis:—
"It is not possible that he should know
More than the wise and skillful mariners
Of many centuries." Another spoke
Objection thus: "So spherically huge—
If it perchance be spherical at all—
Is this great globe, that three years' sail could not
Bring him round to th' imaginable East;
And 'tis a question with the wisest men,
If that the ocean be not infinite—
That it can not be crossed, nor lands be found
Upon the farther side." Others asserted:—

"If any one should sail so far awest,
He never would be able to return:
The world being round, his thither course would be
All way descending; and returning thence
Could not be done without the strongest gale."
And others, looking reverent and devout,
Spoke gravely—"St. Augustine questions it."
"He is a crafty felon and deceiver,"
Came from the lips of others; and all agreed
That it did not become the dignity
And state of princes there to act upon
The reasonings with which the mariner
Weighed his adventurous hypothesis;
And the embodiment of this conclusion
Went to the navigator in this form:—
"Because we are so occupied with wars,
Especially the conquest of Granada,
We can not treat upon the subject now."—
All this is what I did at Salamanca,
In th' convent of St. Stephen's.

BEEL. Thou didst well;
And it behooves us much that we beware
That his persisting efforts shall effect
No voyage following the days and nights
Into the farther West.

Enter IMP.

News to report
Hast thou, that thou hast come so swiftly here?

IMP. Perez, once the Queen's confessor, has become interested in behalf of the navigator, and will be his solicitor for the aid of the crown, for which he is now on his way to Santa Fé, where the sovereigns are superintending the siege of Granada's capital.

BEEL. So perseverance doth impel him yet—
Or spirit of celestial temper rather—
To urge the undertaking of his plan
To track the wide and solitary waste.
His perseverance shall by perseverance
Be met, and obstacles beset him till
Successive failures cause abandonment
Of his designs to follow out the West.—
Diabolos, thy course to Santa Fé
Must traverse speed. Go, thwart the will of Heaven,
If such be there to find expedient
Against the wiles with which we interrupt
Celestial influence: go and inspire
Effective doubts, and such misgivings, that
The mariner shall dream of storms and wrecks,
And agonies of yielding up the ghost
In bottom of the sea; and in such dreams
Drown every one of his adventurous thoughts.

[*Exeunt.*

SCENE II.

Ethereal Space.—Enter URIEL, ITHURIEL, *and other* Angels.

URIEL. The voice of Perez shall, at Santa Fé,
Move sovereign audience, nor shall the powers
That move in plagues and punishment, again
Invade the council—there to disapprove,
With feigned objection and assumptive fault,
The course across the broad sea, which shall reach
The other hemisphere.

ITH. That is our charge,
Which shall be done; ay, we will guard the space
Of the solicitation in behalf
Of him who fain would gather to his aid
Sufficiency to course the western way
Across the wide, unfathomable wave
That marges on the isolated shore,
Where yet shall congregate from all the globe
People to form a nation powerful
To break the manacles of ages dark,

And send its virtuous influence afar
Through every way of earth's inhabitation.

URIEL. How soon, Ithuriel, may we see this
In full accomplishment?

ITH. Six centuries
Shall be the struggle hard 'gainst wrong and darkness,
And 'gainst the cause of all—the evil fruit,
Before the nations shall behold in full
The power and glory of a nation's virtue!
But let us hasten forth to Santa Fé,
Whence, from our presence at the consultation,
The powers of hell shall fearful shrink away,
Or thence be driven by flaming armaments,
Who would not dare again attempt to prove
Armipotence celestial! [*Exeunt.*

SCENE III.

A Forest.—Enter BEELZEBUB *and* DIABOLOS, *meeting.*

BEEL. What gratifying news canst thou report
From Santa Fé?—again the mariner
No doubt has been refused the aid he seeks
To undertake the voyage. Tell me what
Reply to his solicitation made

The Queen and sovereigns, that I may prepare
For risible expression, as thou dost
No doubt expect to move me.

DIAB. If thou wouldst
Distend thyself with laughter, it would be well
That thou begin at once, that thou dilate
With full rejoicing; for when I shall tell
My great mishaps, thou wilt collapse again.

BEEL. I know thy very meaning: thou hast not
Succeeded, then, with what at Salamanca
Was well effected; and I wonder why.

DIAB. Into the Hispan court at Santa Fé
I gained not entrance; for a vasty force
Of thronged celestials armed with flame and light
That made my vision shrink, compelled me back:
Nor could I put on terrors to disperse
Array so formidable, nor affright
With noise, though I sent lightnings forth in shapes
Of hostile armor from the dreadful deep,
And shrieked back on their fast-pursuing course
All clamorous uproar!

BEEL. This betokens much;
And more significant the cause appears
That so provokes supernal opposition.

DIAB. Let us impel them back—and gather now
Our forces from the world and from the deep,

And fury wage against th' empyreal hosts,
And turn their course swift upward whence they came:
Then will I make, with violent discharge,
Vesuvius shoot at heaven, and fiery danger
Threaten the sky.

BEEL. No; brave Diabolos,
We have gained naught in battle absolute
Against celestial hosts: then let us rather
Work on with wiles, wherein is greater strength,
Which we have proved by long experiment.
Whatever may be done at Santa Fé,
No vessel yet is ready for the voyage:
And now surveillance we will keep at ports,
Awaiting there the opportunity
For sudden interruption.

DIAB. Be it so:
I shall rend top-sails, and twist to fragments
The joined masts, and strangle the vessels all
Beneath the mountain-wave!

BEEL. That may be done
If it be well, to know which, wisdom waits
Our consultation.—Lucifer doth know,
And will advise with reaching sapience
What is expedient: the way is best
Which he proposes; therefore give all heed
When counsel opportune from him I gain. [*Exeunt.*

SCENE IV.

A Country in SPAIN.—*Enter* LUCIFER.

LUC. How shall my fortunes mount—how thrive
Upon the drooping world hell's machinations!
My purpose moves upon experiment;
For, from the fruits of th' earth is death distilled[12]
In fiercer and more potent quality,
That makes destruction swifter, and its tide
Shall bury nations in its deepening woes;
Nor can the currents of Redemption flow
Into the depth of hell, though the Messiah
Himself did suffer agonies—DIED?
What if his incarnation hath availed
Naught? This distilled essence shall enhance
All woes! This is the liquid fire of hell!
And on its swift and burning flood shall move
Strife, hate, and death—determinate destruction—
Ay, these shall swifter throng the wide-ope'd gates
Of th' endless and immitigable deep.
Of this, as if 'twere nectar, shall the nations

Largely imbibe, so sweet the taste of death
Shall be to their empiric appetites:
Then they shall drink, and loud shall be their shouts:
"This is the universal panacea,
The emanation of divinity."[13]
Anon the furious deep shall echo forth
Laughter upon the groanings of despair;
And while the earth shall stand, this liquid death
Shall make the soul of man all desolate.
The intellectual spirit shall be bound;
And Revelry shall laugh at consequence,
And hush the very voice that would assail
The CAUSE of hell's enlarged prosperity!
Yet sad presentiment abides with me—
That on the western world will virtue spring
To curb and overthrow in Christendom
And all the earth, the sway which I shall hold
By th' spirit of the still; I must prevent
Adventure thither; for an expedition
In meditation is even now conceived,
To track the sea, and on its distant bounds
Find empire: To prevent this I have given
Beelzebub strict charge, nor know I yet
What probabilities await his office.

Enter BEELZEBUB.

BEEL. Hail, Lucifer!——

LUC. Beelzebub, all hail! Is there more cheer?
Hast thou with thy so potent influence,
Thwarted the voyage that across the tide
Was held in contemplation — is it yet
Abandoned?

BEEL. No: three caravels from Palos,
While now the sun doth his diurnal course
Wheel down the occident, with spreading sails
Move thitherward, and must ere long find out
The world that lies at west.

LUC. Thou art prepared
To thwart their course with interruption dire.

BEEL. By thy advising means: though at thy charge
I have in vain used effort to prevent
The voyage which is undertaken now
In spite of all: Thinkst thou 'tis possible
That we its consummation yet may thwart?

LUC. What! can ye not to their destruction rouse
The violence of the vexed elements,
And split with wrathful waves the hollow crafts
That spurn the lower depth? Can ye not breathe
Into the passions flames of mutiny,
Thus causing usurpation of command;
That the employ vex more the troubled sea
With the firm admiral's unwilling bulk,
Then turn to seek the port of their departure?

Haste thither with thy forces; Break the vessels
Across the waves with strokes of violent tempests!
Sink them and all into the lower brine,
That their adventure perish: or raise mutiny
To cast the admiral into the foam:—
So much he likes adventure, let him there
Explore the oozy bottom of the deep;
Nor will he open then across the flood,
A way upon the terrene occident.

BEEL. It shall be done: I will amaze with danger
The caravels at sea. I will inhabit
The corposant; and from the deck and yard-arms,
And the mast-heads, I will observe the spirits
At my command, what way they shall affect
The mariners, to make them do what tempests,
By insubordination, may, perchance,
Fail to effect.

LUC. Attend it well; for on
Efficient action there depends our state
In most important measure. [*Exeunt.*

SCENE V.

IRELAND.—*Enter* TYPHON, IMP, *and* BACCHO.

BAC. This distilled essence is the much betterviler liquor.

IMP. What name shall we give it? It should have exceedingly good name.

TYPH. Oh, such name as will give the pretension of its opposite qualities—such as lengthen the life of the drinker, and make him feel strong when he is weak, and have spirits when he is dispirited for lack of spirits!

IMP. Then we will call it rope.

TYPH. Why, rope? Can a rope give spirit, make a man strong, or extend his life.

IMP. Yea, it can do all that.

TYPH. By what strange appliance can it be shown to have such qualities?

IMP. No strange appliance: Refractory youth dance spiritedly by the application of rope; therefore it gives spirit. This liquor makes one man cut another to pieces, that he be hanged for it: then rope extends his life into the other world so quickly that he has only time to give a few kicks and struggles, and all is over. And when a man's life, by means of a rope, is taken from him, he becomes strong, and stronger, and strongest, like any decaying carcass.

TYPH. I grant it so; yet we must not give this liquor such name as will remind one of spirit resolved painfully, or of being suspended till life be suspended, or of the strong odor of his returning clay, for it might cause him to pale and his hand to quiver when he lifts the chalice to his lips.

IMP. What name then should we give it?

TYPH. Why, it should be known to men by such name as will sweeten their bibing propensities; we will call it usquebaugh, aqua vitæ, and other terms that denote good qualities.

BAC. The water of life, aqua vitæ: O that be a very good name; for it be verily the quintessence of my being: it be the entity of my quiddity.

IMP. It be a good name for —

While it hurries a man *through* life
He thinks it gives him *new* life.

TYPH. Lies are ever most excellent currency. I have told the great doctors that it is the panacea sent from heaven for the physical renovation of mankind.

Really it shall become so common in future time by Baccho's influence—

BACH. Ay, by my influence.

TYPH. —that every man may prescribe it for himself and friends from palatial instigation, and the influence of conventionality. This liquor shall be common in Christendom, and the Christians shall carry it among the heathens;—so said the great, wise Lucifer, and the great, wise Beelzebub.[14]

BACH. Ay, by my influence.

IMP. Why then do they make efforts to prevent the discovery of the western land across the wide sea?—for by voyages thither this better-viler liquor may be carried to the wild red man of the wild, so he may have full share of the vital-destroying essence.

TYPH. I know not why, unless it be from suspicion that on the western world may arise influences more powerful than any yet, to oppose the good-vile liquors.[15] Yet, we will know all hereafter. The wisdom of Lucifer directs.

Enter DIABOLOS.

DIAB. Why waiting here? The ships are flying west.
Beelzebub demands your presence quick;
So take your course with me to use vast power
To intercept the voyage on its way. [*Exeunt.*

SCENE VI.

On a Ship at Sea.—Enter BOATSWAIN *and* SAILORS.

1ST SAIL. We be very rats to feed the grimalkin, whose use of life is but to eat us; or what do we here? The admiral will hazard our lives that he may hope to be a great lord: if we be not rats then we have sailed far enough in this direction.

2D SAIL. Ay, we have: let us throw him into the sea and satisfy him with wide dominion; he shall have a surfeit on't, then we will turn the course of our vessels landward, and on our return say that our good admiral fell overboard.

3D SAIL. Ay, let us throw him into the sea and return to port again—let us throw him into the sea.

1ST SAIL. Return? Why, we shall never return; for in these seas we will never have a breeze to carry us back.

2D SAIL. Here comes the admiral. He shall have drink enough in his last hour.

Enter COLUMBUS.

1ST SAIL. Where's the land? Where's the land?

2D SAIL. The land—the land: show us the land: we care not for signs; let us see the land: we will go no farther.

COL. Nay, be patient; remember the rewards.

1ST SAIL. The rewards be only promises, and such can neither be touched nor tasted, nor smelt; what then be they good for? and our lives be as little worth for the chances of losing: what will we do with promises when we lie drowned? They will not be in our possession, no; nor in anticipation either.

2D SAIL. There is land where we embarked: we will go thither; and when we become fools again, we will hunt the sea for vagaries.

COL. Nay; but remember, my brave mariners—
Ye who have noted all these signs of land—
What glory shall be yours on your return,
If but a few days more we keep our course
To disembark upon the fairest clime
Beneath revealing day: a few days more
Will bring us to the Indies; and returning,
Joy will accompany; and would ye rather
Cut short the full accomplishment of all
That hath invited us so far on sea,
And risk returning dangers but to hear
The hissing scorn of every gondolier?

BOAT. 'T is yet *a few days more;* a few days more

And then land not discovered, shall it be
Again, *a few days more?* What do we care
For crabs, or weeds, or river fowls, or doves?
They are not land;—we can not disembark
On such vague signs; and yet *a few days more!*
Well, be it so; what then? Shall we return?
COL. After three days, if then we find not land,
We will return.
BOAT. Cheerily, brave mariners,
All to your posts; for only three days more
We go in this direction. [*Exeunt.*

SCENE VII.

A Forest.—Enter LUCIFER *and* BEELZEBUB.

LUC. I like it not: I rather would it were
That mischief on the main had served our purpose.
BEEL. Great were my efforts, yet I could not give
Direction to the dangers of the sea
That they should take possession of the fleet,
And with its course deal with such violence
As to prevent the far discovery.
I went before, and in the air hung terrors
That paled the mariners: anon I roared

Dismal monotony along the deep;
And on their course direct I did resolve
All into flame, and plunge into the sea,
That shuddered with alarmed surprise: above,
In circumambient air, my forces stood,
And swift at my command wheeled down their flight
To their appointed stations on the ships,
Exciting discontent and deep complaints
Among the mariners, with whom they held
Invisible their presence. Thence arose
Murmurs that threatened violence upon
The admiralship. The sea stood ready
To gulp the staid commander: following,
The foam divided where instinctively
The hungry monsters of the deep pursued.
In an unconscious night, the admiral's ship
I guided in the current treacherous,
That it was cast upon the perilous rocks;
Yet all escaped, although the sea did roar
With violent desire to swallow them.
By the supernal powers the furious storm
Was wrested from my grasp, or otherwise
I would have dashed the caravels abreak
Upon the hugest wave or rocky beach.
So on the sea our efforts have been vain:
I have advised thee.

Luc. The Heavens verily
Do strive against us, and advance with care
Upon the West all hurrying design
There to establish, to our much regret,
A nation from which hinderance will come
To the fulfilling measure of our deeds.

Beel. If there a nation shall proceed ere long,
Why not to our advantage? May we not
Follow with guile, and swift pursue the course
Of influence celestial, and resolve
Opposing circumstance into accordance
With our advancing power? Then may we not
Encourage emigration to that shore,
Rather than hinder it, and there display
Afar the ensigns of successful war
Among the civil nations, that they bend
To our full sway; and may we not enhance
Our power upon the red man of the wild,
With good-vile essence? Yet my confidence
Is fully in thy wisdom; and I seek
Not to oppose, but rather know why yet
Our rule may not advance across the sea
With thither progress of the artful world.

Luc. Beelzebub, thou knowest the very cause
Whereby we rule the earth's inhabitants.

Beel. Ay, verily, the entity of ill,

Opposing God and Nature, from the heart
Proceeding, courses in the crimson life,
Administering death and fast destruction
To Nature's call for life, and fashioning
The mind into a rebel instrument
Against the Agent of eternal Law!
  LUC. Well hast thou said!—and, O Beelzebub,
I apprehend, by some presentiment,
There are calamities across the sea
Awaiting us.——
I apprehend that on the Western world
There will arise a more effectual war
Against our power than hath assailed us yet,
And that our rule—which we shall much enhance
By the rebellious spirit of the still,
Which with its fiery potency shall flame
Infernal influence in human passions,
And make the nations subject—will be given
To fearful hazard there: 'tis therefore best
To place impediment before adventure
In every way, and meet with hinderance
All effort that designs the settlement
Of that vast wild by these inhabitants.
  BEEL. It shall be done: I will wreck vessels,
Or instigate the red man of that wild
To murderous ire that shall with violence

Pursue disembarkation on their country,
And, by extermination full, discourage
Adventure more.

LUC. Go; and success await!
Celestial power doth follow Heaven's design,
To guard attending interest. If thou fail,
Then let the warfare come in which will we
Bring to full proof the vasty power of wiles!

[*Exeunt.*

SCENE VIII.

The Blue Ridge, in AMERICA, A. D. 1620.—*Enter* LUCIFER *and* BEELZEBUB.

BEEL. No doubt 'tis by Omnipotence designed,
For all according semblance of events
Approve it thus.
LUC. From European shores
They come in flying vessels o'er the main,
And swell the borders of their settlements.
BEEL. My efforts to prevent this have been great:
I have sent dangers forth upon the sea
To cross the way of hither-sailing vessels,
And have inspired this savage wild with fury
And crimson carnage from distempered passions,
That much has hindered the advancement here
Of lingering settlement to ope this wild;
Yet from the Orient, to these far shores
Come habitants.
LUC. Ay, even as thou sayst,
Thy efforts have availed much to retard

The rising nation here. Continue them,
And stay advancement by thy influence
Over the ocean-tempests and the passions
Of th' aboriginal inhabitants.

BEEL. My power shall there be felt, and fiery liquid
Shall flame such spirit in the savage breast,
As shall essay upon these colonies,
Repelling and exterminating power:
And I will send a moiety of force
To course upon the sea the wrecking tempests,
That dangers multiply upon the way
Of hither-sailing vessels.

LUC. Not of all;
For there are some that may advantage us,
If, on the vexed sea and this continent,
Supernal influence should circumscribe
Thy power, that it should want efficiency
To fill the measure of extermination
Entire to these intruding colonies.

BEEL. The vessels coming from the ardent clime
Of Africa, and bringing Ethiops
To serve the Spanish settlements upon
The farther South, may be of the advantage
That moves thy intimation of regard.

LUC. Not those alone; for there is now a vessel
That, from the country of the Ethiop,

Tends hitherward, and brings a score of slaves,
To disembark upon these latitudes,
And serve the habitants abiding here.

BEEL. Should I allow that vessel to arrive
In safety?

LUC. Vex the tempests not to wrath,
Nor sea to boister anger on the way
That craft pursues, nor any such as bears
The Ethiops hither; for they may advantage
Our full-determined sway upon the world:
For if it shall be that upon this wild
A civil nation rise, there shall be here
Such systematic Ethiopian bondage,
As will, no doubt, subserve our purposes.

BEEL. And yet I apprehend, O Lucifer,
That such would work against more than advance
Our rule!

LUC. What harm dost thou suspect from this?

BEEL. If it should be that, in despite my power,
A nation shall arise upon this shore,
With lumination from the Orient;
The harm that doth resolve, in my suspect,
By the permission in these latitudes
Of Ethiop slaves, is this: The habitants
In these degrees—central between the clime
That 'neath the Ursine constellation rolls

Its icy circle, and the equinox
That makes beneath the burning Zodiac
Perpetual rotation—have come hither
From Albion mostly; and less credulous
Are they of the proclaimed efficiency
Of such indulgences and absolutions
As metal from the nether earth may buy.
Some have from other countries come, t' escape
The utmost tortures of the Inquisition,
With which from heretics do we extort
Confessions, and inspire within their hearts
Pale dread.

LUC. Ay, it appears so, very much,
In circumstance of these inhabitants.

BEEL. And if these scarcely find congenial here
The torrid season, that they may pursue
All needed occupations, they may not
Make to the burning south farther advance;
And we may hold those sultry latitudes
In papal bondage, and in such convenience
Make all avail of opportunity
To make aggressions on religious freedom
In this contiguous clime; and 'tis my thought
That if the Ethiops, who with endurance
Abide oppression of the sultry day,
Serve these inhabitants, they may advance

Hard on the burning zone, and there encroach
With all religious freedom on the shores
Of the large gulf, and on the florid land
Of the peninsula, where now from Spain
There are established votaries of *our*
Religion, which, with torturous racks, and gibbets,
And fire, and galleys, and dreaded armaments,
We do defend and urge aggressively
Against the peace of all the world!——

LUC. Hast thou no further reason to advance
Objectively?

BEEL. We have established customs
In Africa, which, in the language of
The Christian tongue, are noted *barbarous*—
The burial alive of wives and slaves,
When, from the outward of this mundane sphere,
The husband's spirit, from its tenement
Left moldering, hath found th' eternal shades.
The human sacrifices, too, to Bossum:
Yam customs, where the bloody saturnalia
Inspires the adoration of the Fetich—
And shrouded there humanity with such
Consummate darkness that it even grovels
On the low earth! But, from the circumstance
Of Ethiop slavery here in Occident,
There may proceed an influence from out

This hemisphere, to end the full dominion
Whereby we sway all Ethiopia.
The land of Africa, strewed with the skulls
Fallen from the hostile front of savage tribes
Met in vindictive warfare, then might feel
The tread of heavenly peace, and light celestial
Dispel the darkness gathered on that clime,
And Ethiopia look up to Heaven.

LUC. Beelzebub, wisdom hath often served
Thy utterance, which, with expression true,
Hath told the very secret of our rule.

BEEL. Ay, this is th' very secret of our rule:
With vile, destructive essences do we
Contaminate the very blood of life,
And thus develop, in the being man,
The most unnatural predominance
Of faculties, which, yielding to our sway,
Urge the pursuit of evil, and in shade
So deep shroud him, that he will not, nor dare,
Seek light ![16]

LUC. With essences of vileness, ay;
And by this very means man may receive
Our doctrines: therefore it shall not avail
The powers supernal, if the Christian world,
By any circumstance, be instrument
In the establishment in Africa

Of such Christianity as doth receive,
And cherish in its range, the evil fruit.[17]
Therefore the essence of contamination,
Being instrument of death, we must defend
Against all effort that the powers of heaven
Shall make to wrest it from infernal use.
Erst I acquainted thee of my suspect
That on this land, now called America,
Would opposition come, and that our sway
With draughts of fiery and infernal liquids
Would meet with opposition more than wont,
For which I shall prepare; and when the strife
Shall come, then will I make of slavery
Upon this continent, an instrument
With which we may enlarge our endless sway.

BEEL. Ho, that would change the aspect very much!
But in what manner can this best be done?

LUC. Through man's depravity in consequence
Of disobedience of primal Law,
Some shall here use the Ethiops at service,
With such severity, and castigate
In anger, with such rigid chastisement,
That many nations, heeding not the cause,
Will raise the voice of arrogant reproach,
Forgetting their own vileness: further, now,
I need not intimate: the orient

Is dark with shade depending from the flight
Of Typhon hitherward, whom I did send
To the subjected clime of Africa,
With charge observant.

Enter TYPHON.

TYPH. Hail, great Chief!
And hail, Beelzebub—Prince of the powers
Of th' air; all hail! In Ethiop-dom all
Is well: deeds are performed to thy full wish,—
Strifes, wars, havoc, and the imbibing of
Intoxicating mead.[18]

LUC. Thus far, all well.
Upon thy hither way, didst thou observe
A vessel making passage to this shore,
With Ethiops aboard?

TYPH. Such I observed;
And on the giddy top-mast I beheld
Mammon astride, with full directed look,
And anxious, fixed upon this latitude
In th' occident: then gathered I the winds,
And with them urged the vessel swifter on
Its hither course, and it is now in port
At Jamestown.

LUC. That was well. Thy diligence
Is thy reward. Course now the ortive way

And on the giddy top-mast I beheld
Mammon astride.

PAGE 134.

Where thy observance shall respect our acts
Of gaining usurpation; go in haste;
And desolation, linger on thy way
Through Albion, and Erin, and the countries
Of the adjacent continent beyond.

TYPH. The work goes well in Erin: thither I
Make swift my way upon the orient. [*Exit* TYPHON.

LUC. Let opposition come if it may come;
Such preparation shall I make for it
That I shall fear it not; for if success
Attend the efforts here for settlement,
I will bring hither votaries of Baccho,[19]
And Mammon in effective complement,
And give our wiles full scope to overcome
Opposing action.

BEEL. Hither Mammon comes
Swift through the darkened east.

Enter MAMMON.

MAM. Hail, Lucifer,
Chief in the dark dominion, hail! — all hail,
Beelzebub, prince of the powers o' the wind!
It fares quite well with my affairs: a gale
Which I controlled not, helped my vessel on
Fast into port at Jamestown, and a score
Of Africans I there have set on shore

And sold them.[20] To the orient my way
Solicits me, where I have left my agents
Making good disposition of vile drinks
In great adulteration, — aqua vitæ
Beer, ale, wine, juice of barley.

LUC. Diligence
Serves all our purposes; go and perform
To satisfaction deeds thy will regards. [*Exit* MAM.

LUC. Thrive all infernal schemes: supernal light
Be shrouded from the convex of the world,
And hell's dark shadow pall this wide domain,
That the dismayed celestial shrink away!

BEEL. All is at thy direction, which so well
Brings earth to our control. — Whence comes this light
That suddenly glows on this wilderness
Brighter than day?

LUC. See: yonder come celestials:
Let us away in shadows; for, no doubt,
They come to spy all our emprises out. [*Exeunt.*

Enter URIEL *and* ITHURIEL.

URIEL. Thus quickly they have fled that fain would here
Establish firm the monarchy of hell.
They shun our presence save when multitudes,

Assembled from the realm of reigning night,
Encounter on his solitary way,
Some lone celestial.
In despite the schemes
Of all heaven's adversaries, here will rise
A nation from which error will be driven
By light of all eternal Truth, away,
As night is driven by the orb of day. [*Exeunt.*

SCENE IX.

A country in AMERICA.—*Enter* LUCIFER, BEELZEBUB, *and* DIABOLOS.

LUC. In all this region, when the late array
Of warring armies, waged hostilities,
Peace heavily abides.
BEEL. I fain would have
Effected such a strife as would have caused
Th' annihilation of these colonies.
And yet the strife of arms has much enhanced
Intoxication with pernicious drinks
From the West Indies.[21]
LUC. We must bring again
A desolating war upon this land.

BEEL. Whence shall we bring forth armies?
LUC. From the isles
Whence sways the sceptered Saxon.
BEEL. Albion—
The mother-country! Well, that may be done
By our infernal power. I will attend it
Even as thy wisdom shall direct.
LUC. Bring forth
An armament to answer an array
Against exactions we shall instigate,
And devastate this western hemisphere
With arms not solely, but with liquid death
From stills that shall be soon erected here
When such supplies lack from the orient.
Here then shall intellectual light grow dim
And dark; and night shall pall these habitants
Henceforth, so they shall not be instrument
Subservient to the celestial powers,
By influence against the liquors vile
Which make the world so subject to our rule.
War, havoc, let it be; and night eternal
Shut out the light of heaven!
BEEL. It shall be so.
Diabolos, thou hearest the decree,
Which shall be answered by our ministry.
DIAB. War, havoc, it will be; and ruin's plagues

Ride on the rushing violence of flame
By sulphurous discharge from calibres
Of massive metals. Forth from Albion
Armies shall come, and desolation come.

LUC. Go, and beware of the celestials, that
Their interference may not intercept,
And gain advantages from our intents. [*Exeunt.*

SCENE X.

IRELAND.—*Enter* IMP, *and* BACCHO.

BAC. This real whisky—this good aqua-vitæ, is equal to the West India rum made of the cane juice, which we had in the wars 'twixt the Anglicans and Franciscans in America, across the waters. O, the occasion was joyful; for the liquor caused more destruction than the sulphurous explosions or the pointed metal! My revelings there have oftentimes been great; yet, this country bounded by the waters, is the favorite country for me to revel in: I wish it to extend over the whole ball; such addition would increase my revelry.

IMP. Once in the deep I heard it said that wishes do no service.

BAC. I wish them to do service.

IMP. And wish in vain. Art thou not satisfied with the good liquors and drinking customs of the nations?

BAC. Not in toto; for though the propensities of the nations for the good-vile drink be great, yet if all other nations were to abound in bibing customs equally with this one, upon this big island, it would be satisfaction to me in fuller measure. O Imp, see; see in all directions on this island. Those vapors be not fogs from the marshes nor the wide waters, but they be fumes from the stills that mantle this country with the pall of hell, and make it congenial for us. O, this good aqua-vitæ; the better-viler liquor for maudlin satiety; how it smells to my nostril! This is better than the curmi or the mil-fion.[22] All Albion now turns up the nose with favor to snuff the good smell of this good aqua-vitæ.

IMP. The people of Albion be also a nation of drunkards:[23] medicated beer, ale, and aqua-vitæ, work the perdition of them.

BAC. Ay, beer, ale, and good aqua-vitæ in better degree.

Enter TYPHON.

TYPH. How, Baccho, with the good, strong liquors does it fare with thee on this bounded island?

BAC. O, well, well: my revelries be affected with

strong favor. Thy swift way, coursing oft this island, and Albion across the channel, and the many countries of the continents, no doubt hath led thee to behold differences. Seest thou not my greater prosperity on this island? Didst thou not come through vapors contiguous here? O Typhon, look about thee — see the smoke of the stills rising toward heaven! Will it not smoke out all celestial influence on this island?

TYPH. It may; and if it do not hide the sun that continual darkness cover the land, the vile liquors that bubble over the fires will darken the intellect of man and make in his soul a perpetual night! I have important message;—across the wide waters important measures command attention: War follows again in America.

BAC. More wars, more wars in America? Ho, that news affects me happily! The last war 'twixt the Anglicans and Franciscans did enhance my revelry there. I will be quick among the armies. Whence be the armies?

TYPH. From Albion to put down rebellion of the colonies against exactions instigated by the premiers of the infernals, to make havoc there and establish stills over the whole country by cutting off foreign supplies of the burning juices.

BAC. From Albion? Ho, the beer-drinkers, the ale-drinkers, and the aqua-vitæ drinkers, will get satiety in the wars! Thither I go.

IMP. It will please me to see the stills smoke in America. [*Exeunt.*

SCENE XI.

ALLEGHANY MOUNTAINS *in* PENNSYLVANIA — *Distilleries in the distance.* — *Enter* LUCIFER.

LUC. Now prosper the infernals! Here the sway
Of wily influence is supernal dread:
War! havoc! desolation! not alone
By fierce conflicting arms, but the more fierce,
Relentless, fiery, and infernal liquids!
Yet I perceive that yon distilleries
Lack now the wonted volumes of their fumes,
And what the cause of it I soon shall learn;
For on his airy way, Beelzebub
Comes hither darkening the fiery course
Of the paled sun that shrinks with wonted fear
To look upon his flight.

Enter BEELZEBUB.

What further observation?

BEEL. Havoc sways

Imperial; but some celestials here
Do work against us. By their influence,
The legislative power of Pennsylvania
Prohibits further distillation of
All grains.

LUC. And no content in the excise
On liquors to raise revenues thereby?

BEEL. So little of regard that clamorous
The people are, against the distillation
Of grains cibarious because, indeed,
There are disturbers that alarm themselves
Lest that the armies suffer lack of grains;
Who represent still houses as a curse
And nurseries of woes and miseries.

LUC. Such instigation by the powers celestial,
Must quick be counteracted or our rule
Will here diminish.

BEEL. I will quickly forth
With powers at my command, and clamors raise
'Gainst such oppression and such usurpation
Of liberties and rights, that quick repeal
Will come to these restrictions: then again
Distilleries will smoke, and laughter echo
From the infernal deep!

LUC. And ever may
Complete success attend upon thy way. [*Exeunt.*

SCENE XII.

A country in PENNSYLVANIA. — *Enter* TYPHON, MAMMON, IMP, *and* BACCHO.

MAM. Oh, there be very plagues within me now
That need much remedies! If I could see
The smoke ascending from the many stills,
All would go well again; for then would sight
Of gold dispel these troubles.

TYPH. So it is,
That when we prosper, deeming not that harm
May ever come, it comes all suddenly;
And therefore are we startled with surprise.

IMP. If I had been sent to the legislature to exercise my power we would not now have cause for these unhappy reflections; for there would have been no action to interfere with the distilleries, and they would smoke still.

BAC. If any of you wish to see smoke, look here and see me operate on this meerschaum filled with the dried weed and fire set thereto; and while I whiff away the fumes, ye should imagine this to be a huge distillery with the smoke ascending to the sky; this I do; and here is comfort by which I forget that any distilleries have ceased operation. See now [*smokes*] and imagine that ye see men staggering along in whichever devious way their noses, rubicund with alcoholic circulation, lead them; and women mourning for lost husbands, and children piping down the diapason audible for food.

Enter BEEL.

BEEL. What do ye here, infernal spirits,—what?
Discern ye not the vantage Heaven has gained
Through dominating legislation? See—
The fire is all out!—no smoke ascends
From these distilleries! and such aggressions
Unchecked, will militate against our rule.
Go quickly forth and swell the loud alarm!
Make the inhabitants shriek out with fears
Concerning the encroaching agency
Against full liberty in their vocations.
Then will repeal come quick, and smoke will rise
All voluble from all distilleries.

TYPH. That we will do:—men shall go to and fro
And tune their voices into rough complaints
Till every little hill shall echo back
According resonance, and murmurs float
Along on the unwilling atmosphere! [*Exeunt.*]

SCENE XIII.

A country in PENNSYLVANIA.—*Enter Two* CITIZENS.

1ST CIT. What change is in the air?

2D CIT. It smells not as was its custom.

1ST CIT. It offends my nostrils, for since the distilleries have been stopped there has been no smoke to cleanse it by attracting its vile impurities; and I know not what diseases will follow, but I think grave-diggers will soon have employment enough.

2D CIT. I think I smell impurities now that do sicken me: O!

1ST CIT. No doubt of it; and ere long our noses must turn pale and lose their healthy appearance; for soon there will be no liquors in these parts which we can use to make circulation go to the extremities; for this war has cut off foreign supplies of the strengthening liquors, and the prohibition of making them here, will soon work the ruin of us; for we will have to drink the thin water instead of toddies.

2D CIT. And some say we will have no more Indian

summers; for there will be no smoke for them: really I think calamities be coming to the seasons also.

1st Cit. I'd rather pay large tax. I'd rather England would succeed against the revolution than that I be deprived of liquors: If we be rebels, let us be rebels against the legislature which does nothing but acts of tyranny—all tyranny!

2d Cit. Let us cry for repeal, repeal.

Enter another Citizen.

1st Cit. [*to* 3d Cit.] Shall we not have repeal of the laws that make us subjects of tyranny,—what say you?

3d Cit. Repeal of what laws?

1st Cit. Why, the laws that make us subjects of tyranny—subjects of tyranny!

3d Cit. I know of no such laws except those which England is trying to enforce by the power of arms.

1st Cit. Nay: I think not of that, but the acts of the legislature against distilling grain, whence comes the good liquor which is the life of us; for it makes the blood circulate to the extremities.

3d Cit. Our armies must be fed or our liberties can not be achieved: Already there is lack of sufficient food because of the distilling of grain; therefore it is well for the distilleries to have ceased operations, that our armies triumph rather than perish.

2D CIT. Give me enough of the good drinks that help so much the blood in its course to the extremities, and I care not which army triumphs. It is the good liquor that strangles the worms, and cures the colics, and the cramps, and the rheumatisms, and the gouts. In the heat of summer it cools me: in the cold of winter it warms me, and makes the blood flow to the farther end of my exposed nose even in the very coldest weather.

3D CIT. But, does it not any harm?—does it not cause want and wretchedness in the land? does it not evil to the immortal part of man?

2D CIT. O, it makes the olfactory powers acute, that I do smell out wrongs! There be no wrong so great as that which deprives us of drinks—such drinks as do make the nose red and full of healthiness, and fill up the whole body with artificial life when the spirits do begin to droop, and make cares go swift away into forgetfulness so that we know not that there be any cares.

Enter another Citizen.

4TH CIT. My property is all destroyed—all destroyed by legislative tyranny! I know not what the country is coming to. It will soon be ruined; for the people will want supply of the good liquors.

3D CIT. The distilleries are plagues, and thereby our armies are brought to starvation, and the country blighted with miseries.

4TH CIT. Is it so? ha! My distillery is my property; and therefore to make liquors my right; and I will do it: I must live—I must live.

3D CIT. I see no necessity for that, if thereby misery, disease, and death, must desolate the country.

4TH CIT. Nonsense. I will have my liberty! I will have my rights!

1ST CIT. Hurrah—hurrah for liberty!

2D CIT. Hurrah—hurrah! we will make liquors, and care not for the legislature.

4TH CIT. Good friends, we will have our rights in spite of everything—hurrah!

[*Exeunt all but* 3d Citizen.

3D CIT. So triumphs the vile essence of the still,
Which makes the heart of man pursue all ill,
And gold become a god to which he makes
A sacrifice of his own fellow man.
When shall the truth prevail—when shall the world
Perceive that the beginning of all wrong
Lies in the evil fruit which yet on earth
Doth tempt mankind with speciousness of good
And lead them on to everlasting death! [*Exit.*

SCENE XV.

A Country in PENNSYLVANIA.—*Enter* LUCIFER *and* BEELZEBUB.

BEEL. Fires smoke again beneath the vital stills;
Restrictions are repealed that choked their freedom,
By the so potent influence of hosts
At my command, who shrieked along the woods,
Mountains, and vales, against the usurpation,
Till the infection caught the spirits of men,
And that infection grew into a plague
That made them clamor loud for distillation,
Nor tax the favor of their miseries
Sweet in their very thoughts as swayed by us,
Yet made all woful in reality.
LUC. Ay, it is well again in the regard
Of these great instruments of desolation,
Whence flow the fiery liquid and afflictions!
BEEL. But, if this Revolution, that now wields
Determined arms 'gainst oriental rule,
Which at our instance grew into oppression,

Should, by supernal aid, at last succeed
In casting off the rule of Albion—
Is there more probability that harm,
By legislative power against vile drinks,
Will be attempted on our future sway?
  LUC. I will affirm 'tis more than probable:
Therefore the issue of this war should leave
These colonies in all submissiveness,
Lest that our fortunes wane in all the West,—
Thence over the whole globe: they may, if here
We check not in their very embryon
Opposing accidents, if such they be
That would pursue our fortunes, thus to bring
Mischance upon our ventures.—It appears
That Heaven's design would free these colonies:
Therefore Diabolos hath charge to bring
Destruction on these armies all impelled
With revolution; therefore we assist
The arms of Britain, and we instigate
The native tribes in aid of Britain's arms.—
Behold Diabolos, upon his way
Hither, in shade depending with his flight!

Enter DIABOLOS.

LUC. }
BEEL. } Hail, Diabolos!
DIAB. Hail, Lucifer, great Chief!

Hail, Prince Beelzebub, all hail!—The battles
Are fierce to my desire: the sulphurous flames
Shoot swift the metal globes that carry death
And pale alarm into the hostile ranks,
From which loud groans do penetrate the air,
And crack the sky, between which and the earth,
The smoke of war hangs palling all the dead!

Luc. We must not let this Revolution triumph,
Which seems directed by supernal aid,
For the design appearing to my prescience:
Therefore, with vasty force attend the way
Of war, and vanquish all the Occident! [*Exeunt.*

SCENE XVI.

A Forest in PENNSYLVANIA.—*Enter* LUCIFER, BEELZEBUB, *and* DIABOLOS.

DIAB. The Revolution was triumphant, ay,
Nor yet a fault of mine: we all did see
The vapors of the upper air on flame,
Bearing celestials, and their course did lead
The armies of revolt to victory.

LUC. Nor that alone: celestial heralds coursed
The way of nations and discoursed throughout
Adverse opinion, whose omnipotence
Held back aggressive arms and left the West
Dissevered from authority, save what
Infernals exercise; for, what have here
Celestial spirits to do, that we shall not
Undo with almost momentary wiles?

BEEL. Voices are heard occasional along
These settlements, which give expression thus:—
"Beware the essence that intoxicates!"
The tax that has been placed on distillation
Is a significant celestial vestige.

LUC. We must with vigilance beware the ways

Of opposition: we will overcome
Excise, lest it should lead to other acts
Aggressive; therefore we will bring alarm
To all its votaries.

DIAB. I am prepared
For aught whatever that will aid our cause.

BEEL. Awaiting, there are myriads of spirits
To serve our purpose, and will quick proceed
Upon that business when it is advised
How to pursue it best nor fail therein.

LUC. Beelzebub, Diabolos, we will
Determine this in council, though not here;
For oft our consultations have been given
To espionage, whereby some lurking spirit,
Descended here from the imperial heaven,
Did early quite discover our intents,
And swift returned to the supernal Power,
Thereby become acquainted with them all;
And, in obedience to his command,
As quick again come hither with a host
To interrupt us. Farther in the way
Where day proceeds, yet bearing to the south,
There is a cave, and near its opening[24]
A narrow entrance to the thickest darkness.
Thither let us repair, and there consult
How the excise we best shall overcome. [*Exeunt.*

SCENE XVII.

A Forest in AMERICA.—*Enter* TYPHON, IMP, *and* BACCHO.

TYPH. How fares it with thee, Baccho?

BAC. Well, with the many juices to suit the many tastes which I confer on the people.

TYPH. Ay, really the liquors be very many, and many be their qualities.

BAC. Yea, brandies of many kinds, and gins; West India rum; whisky, with which I have so much affected the Celts; and many other liquids, of different degrees of good-evil qualities. I have great influence with these and the many mixtures. I have given out customs of times for regular partaking, besides conventionalities which may bring the liquid of bottles to mouths at any accident of time: also, on all occasions, flips, toddies, slings, and the *et cetera* which includes drams of fairly ludicrous names, summon appetites to the guzzling-shops of Mammon and me, established all over the land; and there, on specific times also, the professions and clerkships dissolve a half-hour in potable punches. I am also in partnership with Mammon as a physician: we cure all, in pretension, with medicated rum, under various names, such as Tinctures, Elixirs, &c.; and, by the dispensation of credibly salutary customs, rum and cherries protects from cold; rum and peach-nuts concludes repasts to aid digestion; rum and milk of kine is the good nutriment for the matron, and rum and opium makes the infant sleep!

TYPH. Ay, and qualifies his taste so that, in maturity, rum and rum makes him sleep in the miry ditch.

BAC. Ay, and soon after, in the ground!

TYPH. I have observed these workings to our favor; but across the wide waters,have thy late visitings been effectual to the full bibulous measure of commandment?

BAC. Yea, yea; across the big waters my oft way, like tempests, makes vessels beware impetuosity, while their top-masts, to and fro inquiet, bend down and touch the vexed brine; and on the Emerald island and the many other countries whence comes the day, great has become my power over the erect species there inhabiting.

IMP. Not always erect!

BAC. No; for I make them abject, and lie in mire like swine.

IMP. Except the grunting—

BAC. Instead of which, I bring forth vomiting.

IMP. O, ay—yes!

BAC. Think of it, and consider how much I inspire the sons and daughters of men, that praise be rendered to me, though not solely formal to ancient custom of festivities where liquors be drank in honor of the gods.

IMP. What gods? None, I think, but the infernals, ruling the world.

BAC. Why, I—I: those gods all be I, so honored in various representation. All Athens was oft drunk in honor of me: then lewdness did triumph over the sublime spiritual of the images which were not then more the images of God. At the Anthesteria, rewards incited to emulation in drunkenness, all in honor of me; and Rome, that big city, did me honor with festivities which marked the progress of our kingdom: so said great Lucifer and great Beelzebub. I have been honored in the name of Bacchus, and Cotyro, and Comus, *et cetera;* and all festivities in honor of me, were celebrated, as ever they must be, with maudlin debauchery.

IMP. Great Baccho, this big world doth nod to thee, and do thee much homage. I have oft seen mankind, with affection, prone in the mire in veneration to thee—which seeing, as often hath affected me with mirth because of it.—I was lately in the land of Erin and other countries of the East, and I did smile audibly when I beheld the great miracles performed there by the juices; and those smiles—mingling with the snoring of noses which protruded red from the faces of drunkards lying in ditches, and the resonance according with children's cries for food—was the terrestrial music which moved me to tempestuous laughter.

TYPH. These things be well, Baccho. No doubt thou wilt ere long establish here the habits of the times when, across the waters, the dignitaries and church officers got drunk in honor of Messiah, and the Virgin, and the apostles, and the saints—whence followed riots, and broils, and conflicts, and debaucheries—all which be pleasing to us, very.

BAC. Ha! the parson had the strongest juices then. I called it Theologicum, and the laymen did send for it, upon special occasions, for jubilees: almost such things even now be here: but on the Emerald island I am the essential god—for there, there be more adoration of me than of any other god.

TYPH. Verily, and the people there have become subjects of the Saxons, according to our ordination.

BAC. They be subjects of me!

TYPH. Yea, and because of which, they are subject to the Saxons, whose rule from Albion has been rejected here in America by power of arms; yet if we shall completely substitute our rule here in better degree, all will be well: but there are hinderances, such as the excise on distillation, which may grow into ultimate prohibition. This is to be overcome as soon as the infernal premiers, now in council, have determined upon the method.

IMP. Quickly now it is growing dark.

TYPH. Ay, the orb of the day, declining down the west, is hid behind the way of Mammon, who is now coming hither. He is oft vexed because of legislative authority in the excise, which lessens the profits of the distillation of grains to the auxiliar juices.

Enter MAMMON.

MAM. I come again; and ever on my way
I am inspired for gain to vex the world.

TYPH. Does all meet thy desire, while to and fro,
And up and down advantage moveth thee?

MAM. The works which I regard in principal,
The making marketable essences
For the desire of vitiated taste,
That bring much profits from distilleries,
Encounters hinderance in the excise

On distillation—which to overcome,
I quick would make all means subservient,
'Tis so obnoxious; and why may we not
Oppose it now with seasonable act?

TYPH. We may not know how to oppose it best,
Until the council, which deliberates
In caverned darkness, have determined it.

MAM. I would the council were at end! Oft I
Have hied me to the entrance of the cave
Where they are now assembled, hoping that
The subject which they were considering
Be quick disposed, which greatly is my care;
And thus have I, that I might early know
What course of action swift we should pursue
'Gainst the excise: and yet my management,
By craft and by conspirant combinations,
Hath sometimes made it little of effect.

BAC. Ay, so; mine too. Excises and prohibitions, by my power, have greatly given way or become ineffectual in past times, while I have aided thee in thy crafts, and thy combinations, and thy smugglings, and thy bribes, and thy many other demeanors.

TYPH. For which thou hast had honors.—Look ye all
In the direction of the council-cave:
Diabolos makes hither rapid way!

Enter DIABOLOS.

DIAB. Hail, devils, hail!

TYPH.
MAM.
IMP.
BAC. } All hail, Diabolos!

MAM. Have the considerate, in caverned night,
Resolved how we shall banish the excise?

DIAB. It is determined that the officers
Of the excise, encounter insurrection,
Which shall be quick inspired. Forth let us go—
Mammon, to thy regarded interest,
And Baccho, thine, whereon is founded mine
And great infernal power.

MAM. I will inspire
Anxiety for gold, so the excise
Shall fail to be enforced because of it.

TYPH. I will inspire hate to this government,
And opposition to its constitution,
And make the law-excise an instrument
Increasing disaffection: thence shall come
The contemplated insurrection quick.

BAC. I will inspire the people with brandy-smashes, and gin cock-tails, and whisky-punches, till their rubicund noses smell encroachments on their liberties when they go about to collect the excise.

IMP. Ay, and resistance to the officers will bring bludgeons into service, and tar and feathers also; for I will inspire the people with such like chivalry.

DIAB. Ay, and such weapons as are used in wars—
The bristling bayonets and shooting-arms;
The massive cylinders that pour forth flame
With detonating, danger-flying death,
If any exigency should bring such
In requisition: I will act my part!—
Now let us go upon this business quick. [*Exeunt.*

SCENE XVIII.

By a Distillery in PENNSYLVANIA. — *Enter a* Distiller, *and a* Farmer *with a load of grain.*

FAR. What's the price of corn?

DIS. The same that I paid you for the last load you brought me.

FAR. That is too little: I could have sold this load for more, near at home.

DIS. That market is still open for you.

FAR. But it was a woman who wished to buy: she has no money, but proposed to pawn me her bedding, which is all rags. Her husband is now indebted to me for grain. He works for me, but does little; for he is drunk most of the time. I sell for money—not for promises which are of doubtful value. Money brings interest: promises tax with trouble.

DIS. I pay money, not promises; yet if you prefer, I will pay you in whisky.

FAR. Whisky is a good thing.

DIS. And therefore should command a good price.

FAR. And therefore should grain which it is made of.

DIS. No; for the tax on distillation lessens the profits.

FAR. Curse the tax! I am down on the tax. Why should there be tax on liquors?—they are not so plentiful as water, and there is no tax on water.

DIS. None; but it is a tax on the gullet to drink the water instead of the smooth, oily liquors which slide down into the stomach of their own accord.

FAR. I know it is a tax—it is a tax on the gullet to drink water; and this knowledge I have bought, too, with dear experience; for I remember once to have drank some water, and my throat became so sore that I applied to a physician, who pronounced my disease an inflammation of the esophagus; and his prescription was whisky with roots in it. He understood my case exactly; for he knew what I dared not tell him—that my malady was caused by the friction of water! There is hope that we will be relieved of tax on the good liquors.

DIS. Yes, the people in convention at Pittsburgh have determined to resist the excise at all hazards; were you there?

FAR. No; I was sick internally with colics and gripings.

DIS. You ought to partake more freely of the healthy liquors.

FAR. I think I ought; for my appetite tells me so.

DIS. Well, I will take your grain at an advance of ten per cent and pay you in whisky; for I know you will do all in your power to resist the excise.

FAR. Certainly I will; for the excise makes the price of grain low and that of whisky high; therefore the farmers have to defray the expenses of the war; and wherefore should they bear all this burden?

DIS. And the next thing, if we resist not the excise, it will be increased to defray the increasing expenses of the government in consequence of the increase of crimes and pauperism. Such expenses should rest on the whole people, and not merely on those who are interested in making whisky and other good drinks for the good of all the people. Really, if such expenses be allowed to rest on the good liquor-business, it would be a false intimation that this honorable business is responsible for the stealings, and the bruising of noses, and the gouging of eyes, and the cutting off of weasands. I say, let us down with the excise.

FAR. We will do that: we will tar and feather the officers when they go about to collect it.

DIS. Ay, I have prepared for that: I have a quantity of tar and feathers ready in the distillery; and by arrangement, citizens near by are ready to assist me at a moment's notice. Yonder comes an excise officer now, and if he should say a word about tax we will have sport.

FAR. We will, most assuredly; and we will see such a metamorphosis of an officer into one of a singular species of the feathered race, that he will not know his own identity till he try his appetite and find that he still loves whisky.

Enter an Officer.

OFF. Good morning, gentlemen.

FAR. }
DIS. } Good morning, sir.

OFF. Mr. D.— I have come to collect the excise: you own this distillery, I believe.

DIS. Then you are a believer, and will therefore be saved.

OFF. Of course I am to understand that you intend to *save me* the trouble of proceeding to extreme measures to collect the excise, which method of being saved, I am sorry to say, I am not favored with on all occasions of this kind.

DIS. Of course I intend to save you that trouble.

OFF. Will you acquaint me, if you please, with the amount of the proceeds of your distillery for the year ending in the month of—

DIS. No; I will see you damned in h—l first.

OFF. No; not if I am to be *saved*, which will be in a place so far removed from the place you speak of, that you could not see me at all.

DIS. Ho, citizens! ho! come and assist in waiting on this officer.

Enter several Citizens.

This man wants tax for making whisky. Let us demonstrate our wrongs.

1ST CIT. Tar and feather him!

2D CIT. Tar and feather him!

FAR. Hang him!

DIS. Tar and feather him! Make a goose of the goose! Let him appear in proper habit! Ho, boy, bring that pot of tar and that bag of feathers.

OFF. Nay, I beseech you, consider what you intend doing.

DIS. That we have, and made ample preparations for it.

Enter a Servant *from the distillery, bringing a pot of tar and a bag of feathers.* Citizens *let go the* Officer, *and surround him.*

OFF. Hear me while I explain my position.

DIS. It needs no explanation,—we know your position. We will change it for you: be quiet and submit, and be thankful that by so doing you may save your neck.

[*They partly divest him, and smear him with tar.*

1ST CIT. That's the way to serve the excise officers.

2D CIT. Thou shouldst have been wary of these times that so soil thy office.

FAR. Man, what a friend thou hast in tar; for it sticketh to thee closer than a brother in time of difficulty.

DIS. While he has a friend in tar, we have an enemy in tar; for the excise officer is our enemy, and here is one in tar! ha, ha! put on the feathers, boy.

[*The* Servant *feathers the* Officer.

Now thy habit becomes thee, for it is the habit of a goose. Will a goose collect tax? No, not of me. Or if thou thinkst thyself not a goose, try the liquor in this flask that thou mayst know surely thou art not, by thy appetite:—Nay, do not refuse a good gift; it is good liquor, and there be no devils in it; for the excise was paid on it long ago.

FAR. Nay, be not dispirited when there is no lack of spirits: drink the liquor on which the excise has been paid, then you shall be high in feather.

DIS. See, he refuses like a goose, which he really is; for his appetite is not that of a man. Take him to the pond! Take him to the pond! That is the place for geese.

1ST CIT. To the pond—to the pond! Take him to the pond!

FAR. Away with him! [*Exeunt.*

SCENE XIX.

A road in PENNSYLVANIA.—*Enter a body of armed* Citizens, *with a* Leader.

LEAD. We have in time assembled to beset
The marshal and his office, which we hate
While he doth use it 'gainst the insurrection.
This way he is to come: 'tis almost time
He is to pass: Look yonder now, he comes!
And if we do not make the sunshine through him,
We will so frighten him that he shall think
His days are fully numbered. Ha! my men,
Now keep your mouths wet and your powder dry,
Yet careful of your lurking.

1ST CIT. So we will,
When we have drawn the corks out of our flasks,
And drank another turn of goodest spirit.

2D CIT. O there is life in liquor; nothing else.
Now I could shoot and hit the orbed moon
If it were night.

3D CIT. The marshal is most here;
And I shall make a bullet graze his ear.

4TH CIT. And I will make one graze his nose, and so,
When he hears danger he will smell it too.

5TH CIT. My mouth is wet, besides, my powder's dry;
And I will make a bullet graze his eye,
And danger he will know is very nigh
When heard, and smelt, and seen; so he will fly.
Careful, he comes

Enter the Marshal *on horseback.*

LEAD. Now blaze away my men,

[*The* Men *fire, and the* Marshal, *urging his horse to speed, makes flight crying murder.*

His office now I think he will forget.
He surely will, if in him there remains
Enough of wit to save him from a rope,
By leaving the affairs of government,
In hands of those who best will manage them.

1ST CIT. And furthermore, if there is any wit
Which has not yet been frightened out of him,
That wit will teach him to remain at home,
And spend his days in drink and quietude.

LEAD. We will go home in comfortable mind;
For we to-day have served our country much.
To-morrow we will serve our country more

By taking the inspector prisoner.
'Tis said a force is ready to protect
His most opprobrious person should he need
At any time assistance. Let us see
How much they will protect him when they find
That they themselves will need protection too.
For this we must increase our number much,
And also be well armed with blunderbusses.
At nine o'clock, Ante Meridian,
Let all our forces be assembled at
The Highway Tavern, there to wet our mouths,
And be prepared to show our chivalry.

1ST CIT. Three cheers, good men.

ALL. Hurrah—hurrah—hurrah!

[*Exeunt.*

SCENE XX.

Residence of the Whisky Inspector *surrounded by a body of* Citizens *on guard.*

1ST CIT. Dost thou think surely an attack to day
Will be attempted?
2D CIT. If my ears erred not,
And an attempt be made to execute
That which I overheard, be sure it will,
And by a force superior to ours
No doubt, if all the disaffected round
In these parts, join the insurrectionists,
Who fain would trample the supremacy
Of law beneath their rash and wayward tread.
1ST CIT. Yonder they come all armed: Be all prepared
To give them warm reception.
2D CIT. So we will;
But see how greatly they outnumber us:
Can we hold out against them?
1ST CIT. We will try:

What if we yield our lives to serve the cause
Of law and government? The sacrifice
Will not be vain: To die is glorious
When life is given to subserve the right;
And such is true ambition, and it is
As well in single combat to defend,
In justice, the true sovereignty of law,
As 'tis, in war, to fight with multitudes
In the defence of a besieged city.

2D CIT. Yet when defenders of the right, in vain,
For lack of numbers, strive against the wrong,
There's nothing gained in favor of the right,
By any sacrifice of its defenders.
In war, it is impolitic to lose
An army all in conflict, rather than
Surrender to the foe: To die in arms,
Boots not, unless some favor to the cause
That urges to the warfare, be accomplished.
It would be rash here to expose our lives,
Against the multitude, without a hope
That we would be successful in defense
Of the inspector's residence and person.

1ST CIT. They come; and what is best, that we
will do.

Enter a large body of Insurgents, *and surround the* Guard.

LEAD. I. Ho, men, what are you doing here?
LEAD. G. Nothing
As yet, although we may do something if
Occasion should require.
LEAD. I. O yes, you may
If such occasion should determine it
As gives to acts the name of accidents.
Under such circumstances I have known
Of persons letting windy passion glide
From an occasion into accident.
And will you here do such offensive acts?
LEAD. G. We may do acts that will offend you more.
LEAD. I. Ha, may you so? Where now is the inspector?
Bring him forth quickly or else we will send
You all where daylight will not find you more.
LEAD. G. He is within and I will speak to him,
That he appear and answer you himself.
Inspector, ho! speak to this army here,
That they beware of doing violence.

Inspector *appears at a window.*

INSP. What would you have?
LEAD. G. Speak to this army here
So they shall not do any violence.

LEAD. I. Surrender all, or else the consequence
Will be the death of every one of you.

LEAD. G. We will defend you though it cost our lives.

INSP. No; we can not successfully oppose
These numbers that are here arrayed against us,
Therefore 't will profit not that any one
Should lose his life when there is not a hope
That th' object of resistance can be gained.

LEAD. I. Surrender, all of ye.

LEAD. G. Here are our arms,
And we surrender.

LEAD. I. You are wise to do so;
Nor would I have demanded it of you,
If I had thought you had not any wit.
Come forth thou bottled-nosed inspector quick —
Thou judge-of-liquor, thou, whose office is
Unpleasant to thy cultivated taste
Alone when thou dost taste of watered liquors;
Come forth, I say, thou smeller-out-of-wrongs.

[*The* Inspector *surrenders with his* Guard.

Now march with us which way we shall direct,
Because the public weal will not allow
Such men as you to be at liberty. [*Exeunt.*

SCENE XXI.

EASTERN PENNSYLVANIA.—*Enter* URIEL *and* ITHURIEL *meeting*.

URIEL. Upon this wide extent, Ithuriel,
What warfare doth ensue, for, from the deep
Hell's wily legions come, and here they wage
Strife to the utmost for supremacy.
And to subserve their purposes of ill,
They have excited the inhabitants
Beyond the mountains to an insurrection
Against the government, and thus would fain
Affect the favor of the evil fruit
In greater measure. O Ithuriel!
Will our hopes fail? See the extended flood
Of error that doth overwhelm the world!
The fiery essences excite to evil;
Thence follow wants, woes, miseries, and death,
That cast a dismal umbrage far and deep
Where we had hoped eternal truth would flame
In purity and light, and radiate

Afar, in lumination of the world.
Is this th' avail for which we coursed the ways
Along the waters, aiding hitherward
Inhabitants to form a nation which
We hoped would yield acknowledgment of truth—
And,in such office, oft encountering
Upon our course the powers that come from hell,
Who, interposing with tempestuous winds,
And adverse, and with mutinies, have oft
Debarred our efforts from effectiveness ?
Is this th' avail—to find constituent here,
Of sociate man, the essence from which springs
Such evils ?

ITH. Verily, the Enemy
Of Heaven, and friend of universal ill
Strives here all zealous with infernal might ;
And his emboldened efforts will not cease
Upon the earth until they shall be changed
To struggles 'gainst the adamantine chains
Which shall be heaped upon him manifold,
And bind him and his power, which ere long
Must wane as Heaven pursues against him war!
Nor are our efforts vain, although at times
We fail in partial from our full intents,
Because the wiles of Hell—vast as the night
In the infernal, miserable deep—

Oppose us: and although the insurrection
Strides bold at west the mountains to cast off
Restrictions on the evil essences,
Imposed beneath the governmental charge,
It shall not overcome authority
Here instituted temporal for man,
In government which Providence approves,
As far as may its power direct for good;
For what is good in the authority
Of temporal laws, down from its source in heaven
Comes hither by celestial embassy;
And Heaven, by many missions here, intends
The execution of those laws infringed;
And that I have in charge, and by what aid
I may solicit to accompany,
Now to pursue against insurgent arms
A warfare west the mountains that divide
Affected faith in sovereignty of law,
From insurrection; therefore I desire
Thy way to turn with mine this to effect.

URIEL. To do whatever best may serve the weal
Of earth's inhabitants, is the delight
Of the celestial servitors. —
I go with thee upon these offices,
And in all duties yield to thy dispose.

ITH. The chief officials of the government

Shall follow our intents, and by our aid
They shall convoke to arms a numerous host.
That shall assert the law's supremacy,
And strike dispersion through the factious ranks.
Let us go forth and soon we shall report
Advancing legions, and the heavens shall flame
With the celestial vanguard, such as oft
Led forth the armies of the late revolt
Against the usurpation of the East. [*Exeunt.*

SCENE XXII.

A Country in PENNSYLVANIA.—*Enter a body of* Insurgents, *with their* Leader, *and* RUMBLOSSOM.[25]

LEAD. Fellow-citizens—soldiers! By a long and bloody war, this country has become free from the tyranny of England, which was exercised by taxing tea. But we have now assembled with arms, to free ourselves from the greater tyranny of our own government, which is even now sending an army to enforce a tax even on our liquors! We must resist that army at all hazards and free the liquors from tax; for if the liquors be not free, we be not free ourselves; for the liquors become a part of our bodies, and our spirits be made up of the spirits that be in the liquors: therefore, if the liquors be taxed, the tax be on our very bodies and on our spirits; and the people who drink the good liquors ought not to be taxed for being better compounded than the rest of mankind, but they ought rather to receive a premium.

RUMB. We shall not be taxed for being so well compounded. Hurrah for the insurrection! success to the insurrection!

LEAD. Mr. Rumblossom, I appoint you sergeant. It will be necessary to drill these men.

RUMB. Get in file, men; get one behind another, and form lines—that's file. All about face!—you are now in rank. [*To* Leader.] See! yonder come men in trappings. I think they be officers of the government. Shall we fire on them?

LEAD. No: there be but few, and they can not harm us; and if they be officers of the government forces, we will take them prisoners and learn the condition of the army, if there be really an army, as has been noised about, perhaps to frighten us from our purpose. But bugbears do not frighten the valiant—those that be valiant from imbibing spirits!—

Enter Officers.

Ho, men! where are you from, and what is your business here, with epaulettes on?

Look yonder, then; observe, if thou hast not,
The sunlight shot askance from bayonets.

PAGE 181.

OFF. Doth come this question from authority
That leads against the government the arms
Of insurrection? First I would know this,
Ere I give answer.

LEAD. I answer, then, it does:
And by th' authority we have assumed'
Against the tyranny of government
In taxing distillation, I would know
Why you are here with regimentals on?

OFF. Look yonder, then; observe, if thou hast not,
The sunlight shot askance from bayonets
And burnished firearms ported in array
Thickly and hitherward: thence we have come,
And on no mission false nor vain, I think,
Thus seconded by numbers powerful
And vast; and thou mayst learn it truly thus—
That thou surrender to th' authorities
Of proper government, and that these men,
Misled to insurrection, quick disperse
In quietude, ere visitation come
Of punishment severe for following
Thy treasonable counsels.

LEAD. INS. So thou seem'st
To know not what is proper government,
Or thou wouldst not improperly have thought
Our proper action for our liberty

To be improper. See: the government
Doth tax our drinks, and therefore they are dear;
And makes th' grain sell cheap which drinks are made of:
Therefore the government would make us poor,
And therefore 'tis that we are here with arms.

OFF. My words shall then be few—'tis best; for where
There is no understanding to perceive
That 'tis not best that most the world be poor
From influence of the destroying liquors,
And all the poor should starve for want of bread,
The law alone will serve as argument,
And it will be enforced by power of arms.

[*Fife and drums heard.*

LEAD. I now would shoot you down, if——

OFF. There's an if:
I know thou wouldst if thou shouldst dare do it
Before the dread array which hither turns
Embattled movement and doth set the pale
To quivering. Deliver up thy sword—
Thou art my prisoner!

LEAD. Well, here it is:
It hath been of some service to direct
Maneuvers in our sportive discipline,
Which we sometimes indulge in to remember

The battles we have fought for liberty;
It never has been wielded clumsily,
In real nor affected use; but now
It is an instrument I do not need,
And therefore I deliver it to you.

OFF. I am assured thou hast no need of it:
But of the manner thou shalt answer for
This thy pretended sportive discipline,
I am not quite so well assured, but think
That it will be suspension on a rope
Betwixt the very heavens and the earth.
Why dost thou tremble at the thought of it,
And still turn paler and yet paler still?
Such is the height to which thou hast aspired.
Disperse you, men!—go quiet to your homes,
And thank the government for lenity,
That such permission now is given you;
And never more pursue the erring way
Of insurrection—never more, I say! [*Exeunt.*

END OF PART II.

PART THIRD.

SCENE I.

A Country in MASSACHUSETTS, A. D. 1845.—*Enter* LUCIFER *and* BEELZEBUB.

BEEL. Behold, O Lucifer! the opposition
We now encounter, which accumulates
Against us, since the while ago a gleam
Of light shot out of heaven athwart the ways
Of our dominion.[26] Here celestials come
With armor lifted high to cleave, with strokes
Severe, our palpable ascendency.

LUC. Yet if the consequence, and not the cause,
Receive the strokes, for ever they may fall,
And yet accomplish nothing 'gainst our rule:
And this by plot I purpose to effect.

BEEL. I know great power lies in the depth of wiles,
Which should ere long be made effectual
Against the 'sociated means now here

Established by the embassy of light
To interrupt us. ——

LUC. Behold what night now gathers on the day,
Even while my thoughts concentrate on resolve!—
Although day's orb is in meridian,
Yet, notwithstanding, real darkness spreads
Apace, which to infernal vision shows
More clearly all the things we do on earth!

BEEL. O Lucifer, the much that we have done
To alienate the brotherhood of men,
Through northern and through southern latitudes,
Delights the revolution of my gaze!
Along the populous North hath want, and strife,
And murder, followed ministrations of
Destroying essence; and the very same
Hath followed in more southern latitudes:
Yet 'twixt those countries slavery divides
Opinions, each in strife against the other.

LUC. 'Tis there my plot concentrates.—This the means
I shall attempt: Such clamors I will raise
Against that institution, that the voice
Against the *cause* of all its ill shall be
Inaudible; and crystalline arcades,
That cross our way, shall all be crumbled down
To solid pavements for the cloven feet

Of all our vast authority to tread,
While going to and fro, and up and down!
Beelzebub,——

BEEL. Ay, Lucifer, I know
There are particulars that give thee pause
Ere thou think'st proper to disclose in full.
The burthen of thy meaning.

LUC. Turn thy gaze
Above in the circumference of air,
And all among these crags where there may lurk
Spies from the empyrean, lest the deeds
That I intend, be early known in heaven,
From my directions being overheard
By spies celestial, which have oftentimes
Discovered to the heavenly powers our schemes,
And therefore brought upon them hinderance.

BEEL. Oh, I see nothing in the air above,
Nor 'mong these crags, that leads me to suspect
That any espionage can now be here;
For, to my view through this contiguous shade,
No halo is discerned which doth surround
Spirits of light; and hereabout the air
Has all a sultry savor.

LUC. Nor to me
Appears sign of supernal messenger
Among this contiguity of crags;

Nor vestige in the air nor on the earth,
That shows late way of heavenly embassy;
Therefore I will deliver here my charge:—
There is a youth reared in this granite space,
With reason sealed hereditary on
His brow, in high degree, whose destiny
May be—if we allow it such a course,
Under the guidance of the powers of light—
To lead this government so that its bonds
Grow firmer 'gainst our greater opposition.
Thou knowest such one?
BEEL. Ay, I know such one;
And many such there may be, but he whom
I mean particularly, is Legree,
Who is the subject of thy reference,
No doubt.
LUC. He is the subject of design,
And he shall be our instrument awhile:
He shall be plied with vilest essences[27]
Until his spirit sink into such change,
That he shall do the acts that we appoint;
And his determined way shall find the space
Of Ethiop service, and appointed means
Shall give into his charge the toil of slaves;
And, by the influence of maddening draughts
Of liquors sent down thither from the North,

He shall subject them to such tortures that
The spirit shall go from its tenement
Of suffering clay. Such things, accounted gross,
Will of necessity be known abroad;
Though, while some means show evils to the world,
And teach the world to hate, and fear to do them,
Yet spirits of darkness make the world so blind,
It ever fears to trace effect to cause:
So, when the actions which Legree shall do,
Be known through civil channels of the earth,
The ministers of darkness shall, with wiles,
Divert the world's attention from the cause,
And let it only dwell upon effects;
Therefore the North shall shrug, and fond amaze
Shall seize the nations, which shall hardly think
There can be other slaves than Ethiop slaves!
Nor shall the South then see what harm is done them
By vilest essence, while they cherish still
Their enemy in draughts of burning death!
They have their institution to defend!—
Beelzebub, to thee I give in charge
The management of this effective scheme:
Pursue it with thy service at control.

Beel. It shall be done: the spirits at my command
Shall quick attend to its accomplishment,
Soon as their offices can serve th' issue.

LUC. My course now turns across the Orient
To traverse our ascendency, which way
Lies in enlargement over the wide earth!

[*Exit* LUCIFER.

BEEL. I to my charge will call immediately
Attendance.—Ho! Diabolos, come forth,
Where'er thou art in circumambient air,
And be here momentary!

Enter DIABOLOS.

DIAB. Here I am:
For, at thy bidding, through the atmosphere
My course has brought me whence my deeds have been
Stabbing men, strangling babes, slandering,
Violating virtue, torturing heretics,
And other things in lateral occurrence;
But hither I have come swift as the light
Shot from the sun, or the electric flame
Riving the air; and my obedience waits
Thy will, whate'er it be.

BEEL. Soon thou shalt know
What I require.—Ho! Typhon, from the vast
Of air, come hither!

Enter TYPHON.

TYPH. I am here at once:
I left the pirate-ship which, with my breath

Like to a tempest, I did urge beyond
Pursuit, and it is safe upon the wave;
And I am at thy service.

BEEL. Thou shalt soon
Know what is my requirement.—Mammon, ho!
My summons bids thee come here quickliest!

Enter MAMMON.

MAM. Well, I am here, and quicklier than light,
Or lightning traversing the storm! What, pray?—
My doings have been all of great account—
Cheating, thieving, selling indulgences,
And the intoxicating juices—also
Pirating on the wet and vasty sea:
Whatever thou wouldst have me further do,
I will perform in full capacity
Of my essential office.

BEEL. Yet awhile,
And thou shalt know. Here Baccho shall attend:
His office is great service:—Baccho, ho!
Come hither, Baccho, ho! come hither quick!

Enter BACCHO.

BAC. Bi, bo, bibulo,
This is the world for me;
This is the world for all of us,
Because it is the world for me!

Here I am, you see, come from reveling where liquors be imbibed; and I am ready to do all that pertains to drunkenness. Were it not for drinking, this world would not be the world for my association.

BEEL. Baccho, prepare to work temptations great.
Come hither, Imp, where'er thou art: let now
Thy way through the conducting atmosphere,
Turn hitherward upon this summons quick!

Enter IMP.

IMP. What, Master? I have come from superintending the drawing of corks, the broaching of barrels, and the bottling of cure-alls; and I am ready to do all special duty.

BEEL. Ye spirits in attendance, that await
Direction, know ye one Legree, whose life
Flows vigorous in abstinence, and draws
But little of its true inheritance
From drunken ancestry, nor easily
Yields to assaults of wily influence—
Know ye such one?

DIAB. Ay!

TYPH. Ay!

MAM. Ay!

BAC. Ay!

IMP. Ay! he inhabits among the granites, and his spirit affects the celestial more than the terrestrial.

BAC. He eschews the good-vile drinks—brandy, gin, whisky, rum, toddies, slings, smashes, cock-tails, and the weed: therefore, there is to me no comfort in his companionship.

MAM. Although he likes the comforts of possessions,
He will not dream of gold continually,
Nor coin it from advantage over hirelings.

TYPH. Nor will he utter lies nor words malign,
Even though his occupation aid such temptings.

DIAB. Nor wield the weapons of revenge or death.

BEEL. He shall be tampered with the essences;
Then will he do at least a part of these:
See ye to it, ye spirits at my command—
Legree shall be a victim of our wiles!
Make him so low and vile, and, by the means
So free at your control, cause him to turn
His travel southward to the land of slaves:
There set him in authority, although
Himself shall be more abject than the toil
Beneath his care. Ay, this is not beyond
The province of your power: and more—make him
Inflict upon his service tortures that
Shall free the spirit from authority
Of such subjected mastery. This is
The charge—attend it well: I will regard
Its consummation. Then Columbia,

And Albion, and many of the nations,
Shall drink down death, and weep compassion on
The victims of this victim; but no tear
Shall fall for the misfortunes of Legree!
Ha! then will Albion, especially,
Thunder anathemas against the power
That holds the Ethiop in servitude,
Nor scarcely deem her drunken citizens
More abject than the Ethiopian slave—
And yet this Union shall be all convulsed
Diverse through latitude!—Go forth: pursue
All this, and great advantage will accrue!

[*The devils raise a great shout, and exeunt.*

SCENE II.

LEGREE'S *House.*—LEGREE *and* CELESTRA, *seated together.*

LEG. Celestra, my Celestra, gentle lady,
Thy presence is my life, and by thy presence,
This earth to me is all a paradise—
All seasons, summer, and perpetual joy
Reigns in this bosom which were desert else.
What if all crowns and jewelled diadems,

And all the empires, kingdoms, and dominions
Of all the earth, could be in my possession
By loss of thee?—the purchase would be dear:
I could not thus resign all happiness
And let my soul become a vasty desert,
In which itself, for ever and for ever,
Might roam to find it all a cheerless waste,
Where all the crowns and jeweled diadems,
And all the empires, kingdoms, and dominions,
Could not dispel the gloom of desolation!

CEL. My husband, I thank you: I am greatly bound
In duty to you for your kind regard.
I thank the Giver of all goodly gifts
That th' world to me is such a happy world.

LEG. Celestra, I regret, while business calls
Me to the city, that affairs compel
Such haste and weary course by day and night,
That the fatiguing way may not allow
Thy happy presence to accompany.

CEL. Thou wilt not long be absent?

LEG. No, my dear;
A few days only and I will return.
Meanwhile the hope of meeting thee ere long,
Will cast a cheer upon my distant way:
Without which hope, my absence, dear, from thee,
Would be a real absence from myself;

For, without thee, my days would all be nights
Closing upon departed happiness;
And life be but a breathing, not a living;
And joys be sorrows, and all pleasures, pains
Riving my heart asunder! Fare thee well—
Thus, with a kiss, we part to meet again
Ere Phaeton hath four times driven round
The coasted sky with his swift chariot
Laded with day.

CEL. Farewell while you are absent.

[*Exit* LEGREE.

Yet, is my fear't it will fare ill with him;
For oft conventionalities contemn
Man's high exalted nature and conspire
Against his reason and his appetite
Through mediate potions of destroying essence,
Which all abase all his sublimity,
And lay both what is mortal and immortal
In ruins! From temptation, none are free,
And dangers oft beset the wariest.
My husband has a cousin in the city,
One Malverton, who had been temperate
Through all his youth; and he was prosperous;
But I have learned that since reverse of fortune
Hath followed his successes he has sought
Such consolation as the glass affords

In its death-mingled, mad exhilaration!
Him, will my husband visit; and what then?
Why is it that my anxious spirit says:
"What then"? So heavy is the very thought,
It is a burthen to my soul to think
What then may follow that will make thick night,
Hang dark and heavily upon the future.
When Malverton, with bland persuasiveness,
Says, "Simon, come, let's have a social glass
And then recite the happy incidents
That gathered thickly on our youthful days,"
Or else, by the presumed consent of custom,
And smiles unconsciously insidious,
He says, "Let's make the glad hours of our meeting
More glad with merry potions; come, Legree,
Health and prosperity be in the future,
And let the cheer expression pass with wine;"
Will then my husband yield to such request?
Be silent, all my fears: say not that he
Will take the first step down that awful steep
Which leads accelerating to the gulf
Of everlasting ruin! no; no; no;
Be silent, fears, I say, that thus unsought
Intrude against all probabilities,
Because he is not made of such frail earth
As yield to errors gross and palpable,

Else why do I esteem him most of all.
Celestra, let thy fears no more close close
The opened door of thy adoring heart
And thus shut out the light of happiness.
Simon will soon return, and naught the bliss
Shall mar that will live in his greeting kiss.

[*Exit.*

SCENE III.

A room in MALVERTON'S *House.*—MALVERTON *and* LEGREE *seated at table.*

MAL. Those were the days of our youthful enjoyments, and it is pleasant to live them again in reminiscence: Take some wine, Mr. Legree.

LEG. Excuse me this time; it affects me unfavorably to drink wine after repast. What may be good for some persons at such time, is not for me.

MAL. I am sorry it affects you so; wine is now the conclusion of my repast: Some other time will doubtless be favorable for us to pledge our mutual friendship. We have seen much to-day: shall we not attend the theatre to-night?

LEG. They have good plays, no doubt, from which

one may be taught impressive lessons by the representation of virtuous and vicious examples in contrast?

MAL. Yes; to-night, at the Notional, will transpire the play of "Othello, the Moor of Venice," which represents the unhappy result of ill-founded jealousy.

LEG. It will please me. I intend to depart for home to-morrow, and the conclusion of my business affairs here, is but an answer. I will return in a few minutes.

MAL. I await your return. [*Exit* LEGREE.] His pale face ought to be colored a little. I suppose he drinks only the excuse for drink—the insipid water, else, I know not how he is supplied with so many insipid excuses. I have solicited him to drink at mid-time between meals, and his exception to this time he gave thus: "I beg you to excuse me; I can not drink at this hour with safety"—as if fatalities were the accidents of certain times! I have solicited him to drink with me before meals, and by incidental favor or perfection of practice, his excuse became only this manner:—"It seems that persons have such constitutional differences, that many may take a dram before eating, while I can not without unfavorable affection; therefore I beg you will excuse me." Excuse him! ha! And now it is not good for him to take wine after repast! What! Is he not my friend?

Was he not the most intimate associate of my youth, and is he now not enough a man to endure the cheering liquors long enough to pass a jovial hour with a friend? And, by refusal of compliance, will he thus slight me on all occasions? Ha! I'll see! There is a bar in the Notional Theatre, where we go to-night. There I took my first dram, and many others, doubtless, have done the same, and afterward, like myself, found it easy to partake at any and almost all times. There I will try him: there I will assail the fortress of his excuses, and I will prevail on him to drink with me, and afterward, he will find that liquors are good without any exception regarding particular times.

Enter LEGREE.

LEG. Well, my friend, I am now ready to take the pleasurable walk.

MAL. The evening being agreeable, as well as your companionship, we will have a pleasant time.

LEG. I thank you. [*Exeunt.*

SCENE IV.

Bar-room in the Notional Theatre.—Men *drinking at the bar.*—*Enter* MALVERTON *and* LEGREE.

MAL. How do you like the play thus far?
LEG. Well.
MAL. Desdemona is a lovely creature,
As she has been personified to-night:
I know of no one lovelier.
LEG. I know
One lovelier beyond comparison.
MAL. You mean your wife?
LEG. She is the paragon
Of women, in my estimation.
MAL. You may not always think so.
LEG. Should I see
A being seeming lovelier, I would think
That being not belonging to this earth,
But had come hither from the realms above,
So nearly my Celestra seems to be
An angel sent to make my life most happy.

MAL. I have not had the pleasure of seeing her,
But I observe you are not what you were;
For in your features there is that portrayed
That doth proclaim a happiness beyond
All that which gathered on your youthful days,
When all your dullest mood was gayety.
I beg your pardon that I have not yet
Congratulated you upon your marriage,
Whereby such happiness befalls your lot;
But I am ready to make all amends
That lie within my power, and will express,
By th' inspiration which this bar affords,
My gratulations.—Now, what will you have?
Here is a good variety of liquors.

LEG. I thank you, and I beg you will excuse me:
However much it may be my desire,
I must not now partake—it is my weakness:
I wonder I am not as other men,
That I may bear, at such an hour as this,
The draught that seems the cheer of many men,
Which would disturb my drooping thoughts with pain;
And I would treasure the succeeding acts
Which will be soon afforded.—Tell me, pray,
This way we did not enter—doth it lead
Where we may breathe the purer atmosphere
Beyond these walls?

MAL. If not, it is the way
Where we may find the spirit sociable
In excellent liquors. Are you not my friend?
And will you slight me thus on all occasions
On which I seek to pledge our mutual friendship?
Can it be possible you are not made
Of the material I think you are,
That hath the virtue, relishing the good,
Which, from the heart, inspires the gayety
Thus made a happy attribute of manhood?
No; no, my friend, if you be yet my friend,
The harm is in your fears, not in the draught
Which has the power to banish every fear!
I have no fear, save that experience
Has never taught you how much pleasure lies
In the innocuous and cheering draught.

LEG. Experience has never taught me that
There's pleasure in th' inebriating cup.
I am your friend, and that I will attest
In manner as determined by your pleasure,
Even though in that I should forget myself,
And minister to my own harm. Indeed,
This little difference, that would divide
Our early friendship, shall be set aside.

MAL. 'Tis well concluded, and you need not fear;
For, for the world I would not do you harm

By importunity against your good!
What will you have?

LEG. Whatever may please you:
I will not use the liberty of choice.

MAL. Good cogniac, then, at this time of the night,
Will favor my imbibing appetite.

LEG. Good cogniac, then, at this time of the night,
Will make our further friendships move aright.

MAL. Here is a compound, and invisible
Is each of its component parts: one third
Is cogniac brandy; and another third
Is my congratulations on your marriage
To her who is the idol of your love;
The other third, invisible, is health
And great prosperity through all your life (?)
And this is real nectar, mingled thus!

LEG. I thank you for the audible expression
Of these which are invisible, O yes—
Although not tasteless, being ingredients
Of nectar! Here is health and happiness (?)
May you enjoy them ever, though the Fates
Essay their opposition!

MAL. It is well
To drink our early sports again—to quaff
The gayety of youth, if that be past:
More pleasures now for manhood! Drink again;

For our remembrances are in the draught!

LEG. Nay, Malverton, are not our friendships pledged,
And our remembrances enlivened too?
Will we forget our early pleasantries
Around the social board, which had not then
The chalice of this inspiration on it?

MAL. Legree, you are not made of such frail stuff
As can not bear a wholesome quantity
Of the soul-cheering, soul-inspiring drink;
For, had you been, you could not have obtained
The blessing of connubial happiness
In such a wife as I have learned you have:
The power by which you won her would, no doubt,
Directed to imbibing, find you able
To bear the joys of a perpetual drinking.—
Will you not drink again?

LEG. It will please you.

MAL. This time my appetite solicits wine;
And here are my congratulations now,
On your release from chaining habitude,
Which nothing knows of the inspiring joy
That with this spirit flows into the spirit!

LEG. I thank you. Here is health, and wealth, and wine,
For your continual blessings!

MAL. Ay, truly said, for when I have wine I have

health, when I have wine I have wealth, and when I have wine I have wine,—all which are comforts that come by wine.

[*Bell rings, and applause within.*

LEG. Does not the play begin?

MAL. Yes, the curtain rises now.

LEG. Let us go and see the rest of the play. What was the play,—was it Hamlet, Prince of Tyre, which I have read of in Sophocles, or was it Macbeth, the usurious Jew?

MAL. It was Macbeth, the usurious Jew.

LEG. Well, we will give 'em 'plause! [*Exeunt.*

SCENE V.

In the Notional Theatre.

Among the Audience—MALVERTON *and* LEGREE.

On the Stage—IAGO *and* CASSIO.

"IAGO. What was he that you followed with your sword? What had he done to you?

CAS. I know not.

IAGO. Is it possible?

MAL. Exactly so; d'ye hear that?

LEG. Not all. What said he?

MAL. He said:—"O that men should be an enemy to themselves and not put any drink in their mouths, and thus impoverish their brains, that they have no joy, revel, pleasure, nor applause; but be transformed into beasts!" Encore! encore!

CAS. I remember a mass of things, but nothing distinctly; a quarrel, but nothing wherefore.—O that men should put an enemy in their mouths to steal away their brains! that we should, with joy, revel, pleasure, and applause, transform ourselves into beasts!

IAGO. Why, but you are now well enough! How came you thus recovered?

CAS. It hath pleased the devil, drunkenness, to give place to the devil, wrath; one unperfectness shows me another, to make me frankly despise myself.

IAGO. Come, you are too severe a moraler: As the time, the place and the

LEG. Encore! encore!

MAL. Really, man be all spirit when his body be made up of spirits.——

—— For our own good:—There be many things for our own good: Such be cogniac; such be champaign; such be marachino; such be juleps; such be toddies; such be flips; such be punches—and while they glow in the nose they make the spirits glow also.

LEG. Ha! my spirits now glow.

MAL. Yes, wine is a good familiar creature, if it be well used; and to use it well is to drink it; wine is made to be *drunk*.

condition of this country stands, I could heartily wish this had not befallen; but since it is as it is, mend it for your own good.

CAS. I will ask him for my place again; he shall tell me, I am a drunkard! Had I as many mouths as Hydra, such an answer would stop them all. To be now a sensible man, by and by a fool, and presently a beast! O strange! Every inordinate cup is unblessed and the ingredient is a devil.

IAGO. Come, come, good wine is a good familiar creature if it be well used;" etc.

LEG. I am not drunk;
Do you call me drunk?
Insolence, away!

MAL. I, Insolence?
[*Strikes him, whereupon they engage in fight, and are taken away by* Officers.

SCENE VI.

A Room in LEGREE'S *House.—Enter* CELESTRA.

CEL. Six times the coursing visitant of day
Hath driven night beyond the occident,
Since my dear husband left, nor yet returns,
Though confident assurance set that time
Of happy expectation, to arrive
Before the last two days, that, heavily,
Have moved o'er my lone spirit sadly drooped.
Why comes he not—ah, why? There is a why!
O let my tongue not utter what I think,
Lest that same utterance should sound like truth
Spoke from afar, to murmur in my soul
Bad tidings! What art thou, capricious time,
That mock'st me and dost make thy moments long,

But to prolong the misery of suspense.
Thy fleeter hours brought me all happiness
A few days since, but that has all retired
Behind his unavailing promises,
Which now come up before me dark — all dark
As night! and gloomy as the shades of death!
May joys not come again? O, if they come,
The idol of my heart will come and bring them!
O Simon! why delay? — why dost thou stay
From thy adorer? Dost thou doubt my love?
Or has thy love grown cold so soon? No; no;
Fortuities have interfered; but what
To my dear husband has befallen thence?
O let my soul be silent of its fears!

Enter Bridget.

Brid. He's coming, he's coming.

Cel. Who? Simon Lègree, my husband?

Brid. Yes, he is at the door; I saw him from the window.

Cel. I thank you for that word.

Enter Legree.

Leg. Good morning, dear.

Cel. O, good morning!

[*She hastens to him and he kisses her, then she turns away pale and silent.*

LEG. Why, what's the matter, dear? I've come
again.
I promised you I would in a few days,
And yet the time I have been gone, seems long
Because thy presence is so dear to me.
CEL. I do not now regard the little time
That intervened between my expectation
And your return, for time is nothing when
'Tis past.
LEG. Have I not come before the time
That I appointed, have I not, Celestra?
CEL. Time past is nothing; you have now returned.
LEG. Yet why are you so pale,—are you not well?
CEL. If I am pale, and if I am not well,
I would that I were not pale and were well,
If my being pale and sick, makes you unhappy.
LEG. What is the matter, dear, tell me, Celestra;
Ho, Bridget, bring some water; she is fainting!
Quick, Bridget!
BRID. O Missis! O Celestra!—boo—hoo—
CEL. No; leave me by myself awhile, I pray,
I shall recover from this indispose
That causes me to droop.
LEG. Well, be it so.
Perhaps 't is best, I leave at her request:
Perhaps too sudden joy upon our meeting

After suspense, has caused all this ; for now,
I do remember, I have some delayed
Returning at the time I did appoint. [*Exit* LEGREE.

CEL. I see it all, plain as the very day—
There is a woful future on my way ;
When sets the sun before the gazing eye,
There is no question that the night is by.
So when I breathe my husband's tainted breath,
And see the feature of his shadowed spirit,
I know my joys are lingering in death—
I know my future, sorrows will inherit.
And that it is that makes me sick at heart,
And turns me sudden pale,—no other art.
Ah me! To be a drunkard's wife! I see
The durance of endurance in reserve
For one Celestra, married to Legree,
Yet from all duties she will never swerve.
I know her love will make her cling to him,
Aye, cling to him and cling to suffering,
For such is woman's frailty; frailty? No:
'T is frailty that through appetite invites
The demon drunkenness. Oft have I seen
Outside my path, the dread insidious monster
Luring its victims into misery.
That monster now begins insidious
To prey across my pilgrimage. Is there

No hope that I shall find it otherwise?
The power of habit over appetite
I know full well, and therefore ends my hope.
No; no: Why do I magnify the cause
Of this revulsion that doth make me pale?
Look at life's better side:—Good cheer, Celestra.

Re-enter LEGREE.

LEG. How is it with you now, Celestra, dear?
CEL. O, I am better and I thank you for
Your kind regard.
LEG. I thought you would be better,
And think you soon will be entirely well.
CEL. I hope so: did you meet your city friends,
And find them well?
LEG. O, yes, they are all well.
CEL. Did you see Malverton?
LEG. Him?—yes: he was
My chum, you know, in my collegiate course.
CEL. He is the same, perhaps, he used to be.
LEG. Perhaps, or—no; not quite: there is some change
In his appearance since five years ago.
Time makes such changes.
CEL. Time and circumstance
Do much in fellowship, yet circumstance
Doth oft pursue alone vast enterprise:

Ay, time and circumstance build and lay waste,
Yet circumstance does oftentimes destroy
When time with deference would rather spare.
Your absence has been safe from casualty,
I hope, in all your journey?

LEG. Yes, entirely;
For I need not except such incidents
As are not worthy incidental mention.
Bridget, attend Celestra's wants with care;
She will recover from indisposition
In but a little time—a little while.
Some business with my neighbor down the way
I must attend to now without delay. [*Exit* LEGREE.

CEL. I rather that business had been so urgent that it sooner would have brought him home to its attendance. I fear the reason of its urgency now, may be his anticipation of further question, the true answering of which, might sadly reveal much that I suspect,—something in his regard, *not worthy incidental mention*, which probably would prove to be the cause of an apparently bruised eye, and swelled cheek, and offensive breath! Celestra, wife of Legree, prepare for events in the future that shall rack thy soul!—that shall—that shall—Bridget, come, assist me to retire.

[*She faints as* BRIDGET *comes to her assistance.*

[*Exeunt.*

SCENE VII.

Bar-room in the Notional Hotel.—LEGREE, *with other* Citizens, *drinking and quarreling.*—DIABOLOS *and* BACCHO, *invisible, waving their wands over them.* —Landlord *behind the bar.*

LEG. Who is he that braves me? It was not as you said. I defy you!

1ST CIT. Defy me? Take that, and that!

[*Strikes him.*

LEG. Then take that, and that!

[*Gives him several blows.*

2D CIT. If there's going to be a fight, I'll have a fist in it too.

3D CIT. So will I.

[*Whereupon all engage in the fight.* LEGREE *stabs his first antagonist, who falls.*

1ST CIT. Ho! help! murder! [*Dies.*

[*The other parties escape at one door, and* Officers *enter at another.*

OFF. What is the matter? Who did this?

LAND. No one here. I know not who. They have gone that way.

OFF. That way, then, we go to arrest them.

[*Exeunt* Officers.

SCENE VIII.

A Street before the Notional Theatre.—Enter ST. CLARE, *and a* Friend *of* ST. CLARE *and* LEGREE.

ST. CLARE. I knew his nature noble, generous,
And yet I think that there is that in him
Which, fiery, must render terrible!
Legree a drunkard! Ay, dost thou know more?
I pray you, tell me: doth his family
Suffer because of it? Why do I ask,
For doth not *drunkard* comprehend all that?
And yet I rather that you tell me all,
So I may not imagine worse than all.

FRIEND. Then know that recently I waited at
The portal of his dwelling-place—the door
Was opened: I beheld!—there a pale form,
And haggard, cast on me bewildered gaze!
A child in rags clung to her tattered garments,
And cried the diapente mournful down;

Anon succeeded in beseeching tone:
"Please, mother, give me bread—please give me bread!"
"My child, I have no bread to give!" she said,
And her lamenting voice sunk in my soul
So mournful, that it drew tears from my eyes,
Which, to remembrance, never wept before,
Although my spirit hath been bowed in grief!
I asked, "Where is Legree?" Her answer was:
"I know not where: 'tis seldom he is here:
Go ask the winds, for they can tell thee more
Than I can tell, wherever he may be!"

St. Clare. Dost thou not think some charitable hand
Hath ministered to their necessities?

Friend. I sent them food: if that was charity,
Then charity may dwell in hearts of stone;
For, had the flinty mountains heard the words
That in despairing tones came from her lips,
They would have melted down, and from their veins
Poured all their golden treasures into need!

St. Clare. These evils ought to challenge such regard,
That they would quick be banished from the world.

Friend. But they do not, indeed; and since they be,
The world doth think it is because they must be.

ST. CLARE. There is inquiry further in my mind,
And yet I will not ask your favor more.

FRIEND. Do me the favor, will you, to inform me
How I, your humble servant, best may serve
In presentation of what you would know,
If it be possibly within my power?

ST. CLARE. I feared there might be darker circumstance
You did not like to tell, lest I should feel
The pain that follows most unwelcome news;
For meaning intimations I have heard,
Referring to Legree, which tender me
The fear that criminality abides
On some of his exceptionable acts.
I fain would learn; and therefore let me ask—
Has there been any crime committed, which,
In the account of justice, would require
The person of Legree to answer for?

FRIEND. Oh, crimes be plentiful upon this world!
They sometimes stare us into dread of them
While gazing on us stern and terrible!
And oft the observation hath been lost
In the complete enormities of blood—
So hath the hand been seen to wield the blade,
Piercing the heart of an antagonist;
Whose hand, nobody positively knew,

And in the evidence it hath appeared—
A crowd was seen—a fight, and many men
Struggling together—and a dagger raised
And thrust—the victim struggling in his blood!
No more. Such was the lamentable part
Acted not long since in our little village,
In th' bar-room of the Notional Hotel;
And noisy Rumor said Legree was there,
And more—for Rumor was severe, and made
The charge necessitating his arrest—
For which he has been tried, but not condemned,
Since lack of proof makes accusation vain.

St. Clare. 'Tis best one should know naught of circumstance,
Of which, when all is known, the heart is sad.
To know a little, leads one to pursue
The facts connected, leading to the worst.

Friend. His love for the intoxicating cup,
Inordinate, is most misfortunate.

St. Clare. There was a time he shunned the hellish cup,
Or seemed to shun, as he would hell itself!
I have no doubt that more than common arts,
Or wiles infernal, have upon him worked,
To lead him into ruin's surest way.

Friend. I think his first inebriation was

In th' Notional Theatre not long ago.
At least so Rumor says; and Rumor oft
Speaks true, though careless in the utterance.

St. Clare. The Notional Theatre? Why, that is here—
Within which is a bar, I am aware:
And there begins the playing of such tricks
As make the world aghast at the effects:
And if there be presented on the stage,
Acts, showing the reward of vice as well
As that of virtue, yet it is my hope
That th' counterpart of what Legree hath done,
Or may do, that shall pain the world's great eye,
Will never be presented on the stage
In th' Notional, unless the cause be shown
That brought him into such adversities.
And since Legree is fallen, who is safe?—
For I know none whose appetite I thought
More in subjection to refraining will.

Friend. The influences that surround some men,
To lead them adverse in the way to crime,
May be exceptive in a great degree:
For one who would be tempted easily
To an unwise indulgence, may escape
The influences to such habitude;
And yet another, fortified against

Palatial instigation and assaults
Of incitation quite inordinate,
Yields to the potency of circumstance
That seems omnipotent!

St. Clare. I can account
For his sad error in no other way—
Which error makes the reminiscences
Of our associate pleasures lie in gloom.
I soon shall be at home, in latitude
Toward the sun, remote quite ten degrees;
And when I turn my eyes again upon
The woful and accursed intemperance,
Which casts its umbrage on the sunny South,
All will appear more sombre to my view;
And oft my thoughts will turn upon Legree—
Oh! Heaven, not earth, knows what his end will be!

Enter Baccho, *invisible, with a corkscrew.*

Friend. The atmosphere is most unpleasant here
All on a sudden: shall we not go hence?

St. Clare. Phoo! the vile air arising from this ditch
Offensively affects my nasal sense:
Let our immediate steps turn from this place.

[*Exeunt* St. Clare *and his* Friend.

Bac. Fu! the bad air that comes up out this ditch,
Offends his nostril in the choice of smell.

O, I see that my presence, though invisible, is manifest to his nose, yet by his nose he knows not that it is I; for the perfume, consisting of the commingled odors of brimstone and this corkscrew, which so offends his uncultivated nasal sense, he doth mistake for some earthly odor. O St. Clare, St. Clare! if thou couldst have seen me in some dissembled shape, so thou wouldst not have known my identity, to be frightened thereby; and, withal, hadst thou known my familiarity with that Simon Legree, no doubt thy inquiries would have detained me long, and, in the answering of them, I should have told thee such a multitude of lies that I might have been in want of sufficient supply of them during a few courses of the day: and the lies that I should have told thee, would have been good for thee—somnific—soporific—that thy siestas would not have regard for Legree, nor any night of thy slumbers, the great things which I with the bottles, do. Furthermore, let me advise thee that at some future time I may overcome also *thee*—overcome *thee* with the good liquor in bottles! There be accidents in bottles, too—accidents which Mammon calls property—and I think that it be well that thou be not long in this world. Really, this world be full of accidents as it be full of bottles. The time is almost present at which I am to meet Mammon and

Imp in the bar-room in the Notional. Their speed be greater than mine, and no doubt I will find them awaiting me. [*Goes into the Theatre.*

SCENE IX.

Bar-room in the Notional Theatre.—MAMMON *and* IMP *filling bottles.*

MAM. I have got most effective instrument
To touch the appetite of all this world,
So I may prove all things by appetite;
At least I have got something in this bottle
Of most exceedingly good quality.

IMP. I think that be rather queer, and much is my wonder if, without any aid, thou hast invented extraordinary mixture contained in that slim-necked vessel smelted from the rock; and if thou hast, more is my wonder what it is.

O, it is elements, all elements!

IMP. O, ho! this great globe be all made of elements, and I think thou couldst not keep even the miniature of it in that bottle smelted from the rock.

MAM. O, there are other elements than those
Essential of this globe conglomerate,

And I have got them bottled in this bottle.
Here are the elements of strife, of hate,
Of murder, havoc, wo, and squalid want,
Tears, sighs, and groans, and baleful miseries,
Diseases, dire delirium tremens; — ha!
And these are property, all property,
Which in material form is alcohol,
With which are mingled many potent drugs;
And they enhance my profits very much.

IMP. O, ho! that be not extraordinary now, it be only common: yet I wish thee extraordinary successes; for I like to have plentiful business, — superintending the bottling of the rum, the gin, the whisky, the wine, the beer, and the residue of the intoxicating juices; and the music that best cheers my labors, will be the shrieks of deliriums and the cry of the orphan's wants; all these be real music to me.

Enter BACCHO.

Ha, Baccho! in good time thou hast come, and no doubt the smell of these bottles persuades thee that the mixtures be of proper qualities.

BAC. Good, good; O, ay! they all be of very good qualities, even as any in the most regarded localities of this world — even the place of my last visitation.

IMP. I know not what locality has been favored with thy last visiting.

BAC. Why, the big island which be the stool on which John Bull sits and drinks beer and toddies.

IMP. And eats poisoned bread.

BAC. Ay, my very last visiting was there, whither I went, shadowing the ocean with my speed, and I have been attending to the continuance of the drinking customs!

IMP. Very important customs; and when they all shall be established here, our rejoicings will be louder than all tempestuous roarings!

MAM. And my profits will be enlarged exceedingly.

BAC. O, think of it! births, baptisms, marriages, deaths, dinners, canvassings, elections, contracts, beginnings, finishings, are all celebrated with the imbibing of the liquors; and in the trades, too, think of it,— the fines, footings, pay-night customs, allowance pots, way-geese, muggings, remuneration pints, drink penalties, bribes, and vast many others,—think of it and smile.[28]

IMP. I do think of it, and know it is worthy of risible contemplation; and if I should laugh now, to the fullness of my rejoicing in contemplation thereof, this bar-room would be burst asunder and all the bottles broken no doubt.

MAM. Then beware that thy rejoicing be not vented; for, indeed, such effect would be calamity because of the destruction of my property.

BAC. And here we overcome the people with the juices,—here I overcame Legree, who be instrument in the scheme we be advancing.

IMP. O, I will have care: Thinking of Legree, I have no doubt that his future acts will make John Bull roll his eyes in wonder while he sits and drinks his poisoned beer and toddies.

BAC. Assuredly so. Even now comes the time that I am to meet Diabolos, and with him traverse divers places, getting up fights and superintending the bruising of noses, and the bunging of eyes, and other good offenses in greater degrees.

IMP. O, haste then!—great bungings come from the bung-holes of barrels. I too must haste to attend to the bottlings in divers places for the revelries.

MAM. And I too must make speed to collect the moneys for the good-bad juices. [*Exeunt.*

SCENE X.

Bar-room in the Notional Hotel,—Landlord *behind the bar*—Loafers *tippling.*—*Enter* CELESTRA.

CEL. O, sir! I pray you that you will not give
My husband any more liquor.——
May I think
Your silence gives compliance with my wish?
O say that you will not! for I can not
Return without this promise.

LAND. Go away,
Woman, nor meddle here with my affairs!

CEL. O, sir! 'tis my affair, and if you think
That it is not, look on these tattered garments,
And on this pale emaciated form
Which has been fed on sorrow till it is
Sorrow's own image;—think of my home
Now destitute of every earthly comfort,
Save it be comfort to look on my child
Clad scantily and hungering for food,
Without the wherewith to supply its wants—
Then know that all this misery has come

By the destructive liquor which is here
Exchanged for all my husband's scanty means.
So deeply in my soul my sorrow lies
I can not weep, or tears would flow amain:
O, could I weep my sorrows from my eyes,
My tears would flood the world and drown't again.
Sir, will you grant me my request?

LAND. No; no.
To my own business only, I attend!
We all are subject to misfortune, so
Annoy us here no more; there is the door.

CEL. I know 't is there, and I will not disturb it.

LAND. Begone, I tell you;—'tis no place for you
Here in this bar-room; so, I say, begone!

CEL. I will not go until you promise me
That you will give my husband no more liquor.

LAND. O, ho! you want me to assist you then,
To make your exit from this bar-room quick.
[*Advances toward her.*

CEL. Beware, sir, touch me not,—there's danger in me!
If you advance I'll tear you all to pieces!

LAND. [*Shrinking*] O, yes, I see now that you are a beast,
And now I see the devil in your eyes.
This is no place for beasts, so go away.

Beware, sir, touch me not,— there 's danger in me!
If you advance I'll tear you all to pieces!

PAGE 228.

CEL. No place for beasts? Have I not read the sign—
Entertainment for man and beast—

LAND. Then go into the stable; that's the place
We keep the beasts in,—go into the stable!

CEL. Ha! who are you? Whence your authority
That gives its utterance in such command?
No doubt you give such order to the beasts
You make of men with these vile liquors here.
O, I know who you are—and now my eyes
Are quick compelled to weeping!

LAND. Yes, they are,
And so your sorrows will be wept away.

CEL. If now these tears flowed forth from sorrow's depths,
They might give me relief, but they do not.

LAND. Why do you weep then, if 'tis no relief?

CEL. My eyes do pain me, therefore I do weep.

LAND. O, do they so? Well, I know why it is,—
It is from looking into others' business.

CEL. There is a devil in my eyes, Oh! Oh!
And that's the reason they do pain me so.

LAND. Ha! that I told you, which you have confessed.
I knew I saw the devil in your eyes.

CEL. How faithful are the mirrors of my eyes

That you can look in them and see the devil;
For they reflect the image of yourself!
O, I know who you are! you are the devil—
That is according to your own confession;
And well your deeds approve it: I will not
Pray to the devil, no; no favors will I ask
Of you; for you are from the nether deep.
I will go home and say I 've seen the devil,
Who tempts the world still with the evil fruit!

[*Exit.*

LAND. Ha! I would rather be the devil really, so I could keep all the women in such fear of me that I should get rid of their annoyances; yet, I have now got so used to their whinings that all the feminine prayers and tears in this world shall not work against this liquor business that pays so well. I have made a great deal of money out of Legree; Why, he would spend money in treating as if it grew in his way; and now, though it is scarce with him, I know that what he gets will come into my hands, though his family starve!—but it matters not to me where he gets his money,—when it is mine, it is all the same. He will be able to endure a great deal of liquor yet; for he has a big arm, and firm gait when he is sober. Heigh O! money makes the mare to go. [*Exit.*

SCENE XI.

In LEGREE'S *House.—Enter* CELESTRA *and* Child.

CHILD. Ma, give me bread—ma, give me bread!
CEL. Sleep yet a little longer, my dear child,
Until your papa come and bring us bread.
[Child *sleeps.*
Oh! why does he delay to bring us food,
That we with cold and hunger may not die?
I would have gone myself to purchase bread,
But maladies have fastened on my frame,
Brought to me by my many miseries;
Therefore, some little money, I had earned
By toils severe, I did intrust him with,
Exhorting scrupulous expenditure
For our immediate necessities:
But no return comes to supply our wants!
Nor need I wonder why: too well I know
He hath been waylaid by his appetite
For the destroying beverage of hell!
And it seems, therefore, death awaits us here

By cold and hunger, ere the night withdraw
To let another day awake the world.
Before the morrow dawn, my child will sleep
A sleep so deep, no dreams of agonies
From piercing want, will then disturb its rest!
Then will I rather leave this painful world;
For now my life is living on itself—
It feeds on this emaciated form!
To die is but to leave this famished clay,
And live upon bread of Eternal Life!
Yet why may I not live the during while
Allotted for the habitants of earth,
And feel the happiness the world affords
To those respected by its partial favor?
But I must live on miseries awhile,
And, living on them, I shall starve to death!
Is this the fate that must attend my life?
Inexorable Fate! I would be free
From thy dread power. Oh! why was the earth
Made to possess a little happiness,
Alluring mortals into misery?
Oh! why was ever such a thing as love?
Oh! why the pleasures of association?
Oh! why one moment of domestic peace
To give enjoyment, to be pricked so deep
With thorns of sorrow, expectations failed,

And hopes all blasted to imbittered woes,
That the whole soul must ache?—And still I love—
I love Simon Legree; for 'tis not he—
It is an accident—that tortures me
And my dear child with cold and hunger now,
Through his neglect that leaves us destitute
Of what to comfort would administer,
While he provides sole for his appetite
Perverted to the thirst for liquid fire!
Oh! why should appetite be so depraved,
That one should drink down fire into the soul,
To burn it to a wreck? Ah! there can be
No other wreck so direful in creation,
As that of the Creator's greatest work.
My husband!—the first time I uttered it,
The fond appellative, upon my tongue,
Thrilled happily my soul! still sweet, yet bitter
In this sad circumstance where wretched want
Accompanies the way of life thus drear—
And ruin follows on his habitude!

CHILD. [*Awaking.*] Ma, give me bread!

CEL. My child, I have no bread!

CHILD. Ma, give me bread—ma, give me bread!

CEL. I have no bread, my child; I have no bread!

CHILD. I am cold, mother—I am cold!

CEL. I know thou art, my child; yet I have not

The wherewithal to clothe thee, nor obtain
Protection from these rude and chilly winds
That enter through the broken window here.
Be patient yet a little longer, child —
Then will the journey of our life be ended,
And we will leave this world to dwell in heaven.

CHILD. Is there bread in heaven, mother?

CEL. There we will never want for bread of life!

CHILD. Will it be warm in heaven, mother?

CEL. There we will never suffer with the cold;
For it will be warm there.——

CHILD. I wish to be in heaven, mother?

CEL. My child, we soon will be in heaven,
Where wants will never come. [Child *sleeps.*

Enter LEGREE.

LEG. I say, old woman, where is that money that you spun for? I want it.

CEL. I have it not; I gave you all I had
Some time ago, for you to purchase bread
To nourish my sick frame and this dear child,
But you forgot to do so, I suppose;
For your return has been delayed till now,
And I perceive that you have brought no bread!

LEG. I say, woman, 'tis no use complaining: I want the money, if there is any.

CEL. If there be any here, I know it not.
I too have wants that must soon be supplied,
Or else this child and I shall leave this world;
For cold and hunger prey upon our lives!

LEG. Nonsense! I say, old woman, I know you too well. There's no danger o' your dyin': I've lived with ye long enough to know ye couldn't be froze nor starved. Ye're tougher'n a b'iled owl, or I'd a' got rid o' ye long ago.

CEL. If that can be your wish, then strike me dead,
So you may have the comfort of my absence.

LEG. No, I won't; for if ye be most froze and starved, ye will die soon without my killing ye. I was near being hanged once, because it was said that I killed a man. So I will see ye die, but I will not kill ye.

CEL. No, not with blows, and yet will you with words
Tormenting, drive my spirit forth to seek
A better place to dwell in than this world,
Which seems to me so much like dreadful hell! —
Yet there's no fire here, nor smell of sulphur,
And all is cold: therefore this is not hell!
And thou art not the devil! Why dost thou then
Strive to torment me so? Oh! why art thou
Less friendly than these broken windows are,

Through which the pointed shafts of frozen winds
Fly hitherward, and pierce me through and through?
But now thy words are ruder in attack,
Whereby they fall like lightning on my soul,
To drive it forth from this fast-failing temple!
My child, my child—oh! it is cold in death!—
Yet this was but its mortal tenement,
Whose habitant, immortal, now has gone
To bask in the eternal light of heaven!
And there will cold and hunger never come.
O, I will follow thee, belovéd child!—
My soul goes forth upon my sighing breath,
To happy realms beyond the gate of death! [*Dies.*

LEG. O, I understand ye! Playing possum again, ha? Tryin' to make me think ye are dead, as ye did once when I kicked ye, and ye turned pale, and pretended to faint; but ye got over it again, and so ye will this time.—Well, you do look like a dead person, that's a fact! Speak, wife! where is the rest of—where is—— Will you have some bread, wife? Wake up, wife! I want you to tell me something.—She does not move. Really, I believe she is dead; and this child, too—is dead! What strange feeling is this that now possesses me?——

Who am I? or whence comes this sudden change,
That startles me with the realities

Of my afflictive errors that have thrived
On yielding appetite, whence my affections
Were so estranged, that, with my cruelties,
Celestra I have driven from this earth,
And the sole child that had so base a father!
Celestra, come back to this world again!—
O my Celestra, come, and I will love you!
For I did love you once, though since, that flame
Seemed quenched entirely by the beverage
Which is hell's mischievous material fire,
That burns the soul with everlasting flame!
Celestra, I did love you once; though since,
That flame of love burned low and almost out,
Or quite extinguished, yet some latent sparks
Still lingered in my heart, which blaze again
Now thou art gone from me. Oh! gone for ever!
Now thy perfections show thou art an angel,
And I am startled into apprehension
Of the realities of what I am—
Fast sinking through the earth to dreadful hell!
O my Celestra, I have murdered thee
And our sole child, with harshest cruelties!
Yet, ere I murdered thee, myself I murdered,
And by that crime became an instrument
To torture thee till thou hast left the world!
Will Heaven forgive my crimes so multiplied?

In this defilèd temple of my soul
There is no faith which can look up to Heaven;
For Heaven hath this decreed: "No drunkard shall
Enter the realms of bliss!" Therefore I know
That I shall never more see my Celestra!
And yet I do her wrong to call her mine;
For death has now annulled that claim—O, no!
Not death: the wrongs which I had done to her,
Long since had set aside my claim to one
Who ought to dwell in heaven—not with me.
Oh! why do now these truths break on my soul,
To show how low the depth where I have fallen?
For, knowing of my aggravated deeds,
Will never make Celestra mine again—
To feel my baseness, will not raise the dead!
Then why should I not drain the cup again,
And drown my sorrows in forgetfulness?
And then I shall not know how vile I am.
No: if I have the power to refrain,
I rather will live on in punishment,
Than make addition to my degradation.
Yet from such punishment may I not flee?
Although I can not wander from myself,
That I may thus get farther from remorse,
Yet I will follow to their burial,
Celestra and my child, and not return

Then to this home—oh! it is desolate!—
And I will rather wander o'er the earth,
And so forget that once I had a home
And a companion who was such an angel:
Or, if I ever must remember this,
Then let the flaming armory of storms—
Jove's thunderbolts in missive fire—attend
The utter embassy to minister
Upon me torments!—or else let me starve
In fire or ice, with dainties in the reach
Of my stern-gazing eyeballs! but let not
Conscience be my tormentor! O Celestra!—
But my strength fails.——Is not this all a dream?
If not, then is it not miraculous
That I should feel the love of temperate youth
Burning again the moment she is gone
Into the high and happy realms beyond
The influence of unavailing love?
The portals of my eyes are now weighed down
With an oppression reaching to my spirit,
And I would fain sleep off this heaviness,
If dreadful dreams would not affright my soul!
Dreams or no dreams, perforce I can not choose:
Where shall I lie, save by this lifeless body?

[*Lies down by* CELESTRA.

Enter BACCHO *and* IMP.

BAC. [*To* LEGREE.] I gave thee not that spell, which makes thee condemn the good juices. I will take all the anti-imbibing disposition out of thee.—Go, Imp, quick to the estuary not far, and bring to me a reed hither.

IMP. I am Beelzebub's servant—not thine.

BAC. Beelzebub will smite thee with thunders if thou do not assist me.

IMP. Oh! oh! I will get thee a reed. [*Exit.*

BAC. Imp, that little devil, is notional at times, and likes not to obey when I command. Really, he ought to know, and he will yet learn, that I have more influence on this world than all the other devils. [*Takes a flask from* LEGREE'S *pocket.*] Empty, ha? Well, I will quick effect the filling of it. [*He fills it by conjuration.*] There, that will make thy appetite rejoice when thou dost taste it! [*Places it back in* LEGREE'S *pocket.*]

Enter IMP, *with a reed.*

IMP. Here is the reed,
A tube indeed;
And if you ever knew it,
I could blow a hurricane through it!

BAC. Do not that; for the reed being crooked, the hurricane would form whirlwinds, traversing the whole wide earth: and the danger would be, that thereby all distilleries would be, in fragments, scattered afar.

IMP. O, then, I will not blow a tempest!—but this reed is well fitted for tunes. [BACCHO *takes the reed.*] I breathed music through it on my way hither. Did ye not hear it rolling along on the breeze?

BAC. I heard it not. What kind of music was it?

IMP. O, it must have been crooked music, that it took a wry course, and did not come to ye; therefore ye could not hear it!

BAC. Beware thy wind, lest it should do thee harm. —And now, O reed! grown for other purpose than that of giving passages of music, I will make exceedingly good use of thee. [*Places the reed to* LEGREE'S *ear, and chants through it*]:—

O, whisky is the goodly juice
  To banish care,
  And health repair:
It has been made for mortals' use,
And leaves for ills no more excuse
Upon this world, or anywhere.

It cools the hot and warms the cold,
  And drives all pain

From earth amain:
It never lets a man grow old,
Nor half its blessings can be told—
The cup, then, let him ever drain!

It oils the wheels of lazy life,
And makes all gay
Both night and day——

There, this reed is split!

IMP. Verily, it is because those big lies could not pass through at the joints.

BAC. Hush! What if he were to awake, and hear thee call them lies?—for, whatever they be, they shall be palatable truths to Legree. There—he awakes!—let us be invisible. [LEGREE *awakes.*

LEG. That was a queer dream I had. I begin to feel thirsty while thinking of it; but there's no use of being thirsty when my flask is empty, and no prospect of its being filled. [*Takes out his flask.*] Why, it is full now: I thought I had drunk it dry—dry as I be—but it seems I didn't; else, how could it be full now? [*Drinks and sings*]:—

O, whisky is the goodly juice
To banish care,
And health repair:

It has been made for mortals' use,
And leaves for ills no more excuse
Upon this world, or anywhere.

It cools the hot and warms the cold,
And drives all pain
From earth amain:
It never lets a man grow old,
Nor half its blessings can be told—
The cup, then, I will ever drain!

It oils the wheels of lazy life,
And makes all gay
Both night and day——

Why, I've forgot the rest, or else that is all of it.

BAC. And makes one happy when his wife
Is dead: nor knows, when plagues are rife,
That any ever cross his way!

LEG. What's that? Who is that speaking, and where is he? [*Looks all above and around; then puts his ear to the bottle, and listens.*] I hear a noise: I believe there be devils in this bottle! [*Examines it carefully at the light; and* IMP *and* BACCHO, *getting in range, are discovered to him through the flask.*] Oh! there be devils in this flask—devils!—
I will never touch the bottle again! [*Throws it away, and exeunt.—Thunders and lightnings.*

SCENE XII.

On a Flat-boat at the Landing at CINCINNATI.—
Enter Pilot.

PILOT. I have only Stokes with me, and I need another hand to help run this boat; for there are many snags down in the Mississippi. Yonder comes a man from the boat just above, and I'll bet a treat he wishes to engage a trip. I will pretend that I do not care for more help and so get him cheap, if he wishes to hire. I know they want no more help on the boat above.

Enter LEGREE.

LEG. Are you the pilot of this boat?

PILOT. I am.

LEG. Do you want to engage a hand to go down the river?

PILOT. No, I believe not; perhaps you can engage to go on the boat above.

LEG. No; I have just been there;—they are supplied with help: How much will you give me to go down with you?

PILOT. If I were in want of a hand, I would pay

you a fair price; but, under the circumstances, the price which I should offer you, would be so little, that you would have as much reason to be offended, as I to expect that you would accept my offer; but if you desire to go very much, you can set a price on your labor, and if it be low enough to suit my convenience, I will hire you for accommodation.

LEG. I am travelling westward—southward—most any direction it happens, and I am not particular about the price. I will go down with you for ten dollars.

PILOT. Why, a man who wishes to travel and see his friends, will go with me for half that amount.

LEG. Friends—friends!—If I had friends, I would not be here; I would not have gone so far from home;—Home,—I have no home!

PILOT. Why, most people have both home and friends; yet some who deserve both, may be so unfortunate as to have neither.

LEG. I had a home when I had a wife, and she was my friend; but she is dead! I had a child too,—it is dead! I will go down with you for five dollars.

PILOT. Well, you may consider yourself hired. Will you take a drink?

LEG. No, I think not; I determined not to drink any more.

PILOT. Ho, nonsense! you had better take a little, —just enough to forget that your wife and child are dead; you will find a friend in liquor.

LEG. Why, then, I might forget too that I wish to go down the river.

Enter BACCHO, *and he waves a wand over* LEGREE.

PILOT. Never mind, I have got an article aboard as good as ever rinsed the cobwebs down a man's throat. Halloo, Stokes!

STOKES. [*Within.*] Halloo yourself! what d'ye want?

PILOT. Bring up that flask of the good O-be-joy-ful.

Enter STOKES.

STO. Here it is,—the repose of weariness, the comfort of sorrow, and the essence of jollity.

PILOT. And the consolation of this world where we poor mortals dwell. Stranger, what may I call your name?

LEG. My name is Legree.

PILOT. Well, Mr. Legree, this will give you joy. Take a swig.

LEG. Here is luck for you. [*Drinks.*]

PILOT. And here is your health, Mr. Legree, and the hope that we will have favorable winds which make light work for boatmen. [*Drinks.*]

STO. And here is the hope that, if we should strike a snag and sink, all the barrels aboard will bu'st, so that we will drown decently in liquor instead of the muddy Mississippi. [*Drinks.*] [*Exit baccho.*

PILOT. All ready. Loose the cable from the shore — take in the cable. Row out the forward end, — left forward. All right: here we go.

PILOT *and* STOKES. [*Singing.*]

"Heigh-o, the boatmen row
'Way down the river on the O-hi-o.
Heigh-o, the boatmen row
'Way down the river on the O-hi-o.
Boatmen dance; boatmen sing;
Boatmen up to any thing:
Boatmen dance; boatmen sing;
Boatmen up to any thing."

[*The boat moves away.*

SCENE XIII.

A Forest in MISSISSIPPI.—*Enter several* Land-Pirates.

2D PIR. Are you sure that nearly all the cargo of that flat-boat is sold; for really I do n't like to kill a man without the prospect of getting a good sum of money?

1ST PIR. Sure of it? Why, can't I see? I was aboard to-day, and there were only a few barrels left, and at first there must have been a thousand.

2D PIR. It gives me fear to kill a man, but we will have to dispatch them: When the eye of desire is looking for gold, the eye of conscience winks at the deed that gets it.

1ST PIR. Of course we will dispatch them; "The dead tell no tales," and what is it to kill a man even though the reward for it should be little?—Accidents kill men, and why may not a dagger?

2D PIR. Why, then, only because a dagger is not an accident.

1ST PIR. Well, if it takes the place of one, it is

all the same: furthermore, there is that in this flask which will banish all fears and remorses,—a friend, by the aid of which, I have many times taken the life of a man for but a little money: Here, take another swig: I think you need a little more preparation for the dangerous part of the business we follow. [*Second Pirate drinks.*] There, now. How do you feel?—where now is your conscience?

2D PIR. It is gone, and the liquor has taken its place. I could kill a hundred men; I hope there be a hundred aboard that boat; be there not a hundred?

1ST PIR. No; not a hundred; there be only three,—all red-nosed fellows though, and one of them big and burly, who, no doubt, would show hard fight if we should awake him in this world; but we must take care for that, and dispatch them all so that they shall awake only in another world!

2D PIR. I care not to think of another world, if I am ever to go there—unless there be plenty of money and whisky in it.

1ST PIR. Why, we be in this world now, and we have nothing to think of but the affairs of it. I think it is time now that the boatmen be asleep. Let us proceed on the scent of money. [*Exeunt.*

SCENE XIV.

On a Flat-boat landed at the shore of the MISSISSIPPI River, *far down.—Enter* Pilot, LEGREE, *and* STOKES.

STO. Well, Pilot, how did you like that one-horse town?

PILOT. I liked the town well enough,—but I know not why you call it a one-horse town.

STO. O, I see! Liquor dealers generally estimate the size of a town by the number of red noses they see in it.

PILOT. Whether it be large or small, is not now my care: I did not like the looks of those men who came aboard to-day.

STO. O, I reckòn you think they be ruffians that have danger in them; but I fear them not half so much as I fear these musketoes that now make battle and take from me my very life-blood in spite of me.

PILOT. It is the whisky in you which they are after; you should not drink quite so much of it, but, to be relieved of them, you may both go to your births, and while you sleep, each of you, keep an ear directed upward, and if I should call you, listen to me instead of the snoring that you will make—then get you up quickly and come forth with your weapons in readiness, as if you expected to fight panthers; for dangerous animals sometimes visit flat-boats.

STO. We will, sir; come, Legree, let's take a snooze.

LEG. A snooze is a good thing at this time, but a swig is at any time better than a snooze.

STO. I know it is, for it is a truth so true that I can even smell it by merely putting my nostril to the mouth of this flask. [*They drink and exeunt.*

PILOT. I would like to drink too, but the presentiment which I have, that all is not safe hereabout, gives me a kind of fear that somewhat takes away my appetite for whisky; but what a fool am I to let appetite be surrendered to fear; and what a strange thing is fear too, if it be a thing at all; yet it can not be touched, nor tasted, nor smelt; therefore I think it be nothing,—or nothing more than the vapidity of the brain from the want of fumes of whisky, which, when it is drank, is changed into the genuine spirit of a man. O, I know what fear is—it is the want of whisky fumes in the brain! so I'll take a little swig, though I have no appetite for it, then will my fear be gone and my appetite be come. [*Drinks.*] Now my fear is gone so I think I would n't be afeard even of the devil, if he should appear to me now with his cloven feet, and crooked horns, and long, barbed tail, and eyes of fire, and brimstone smoke coming out of his nostrils—no; I would n't be afeard even of the devil. Ho! who comes there?

Enter several Land-pirates.

1st Pir. Strike him down—strike him down!

Pilot. Ho, Stokes! Legree! come here quick.

Enter Stokes *and* Legree.

[*The* Pirates *make attack—all engage in fight in which all are killed except* Legree.

Leg. I left alone? The result of this fight would have been good if none but the ruffians had been killed; yet why may it not be better as it is. Ha! The money is now mine, and I'll have more than five dollars for this trip. [*Searches their pockets and rolls them overboard.*] The moon is up, I'll untie the cable, and be off with this boat; and at convenient time I will be in possession of a plantation and niggers somewhere in these lower latitudes, and then be as much a lord as any one that has authority. Heigh-ho! [*He unties the cable and the Boat moves away.*

O murder! I am stabbed!

Page 253.

SCENE XV.

Bar-room in a Tavern in the South.—Citizens *drinking at the bar.*—ST. CLARE, *reading a paper.*

1ST CIT. Come, St. Clare, take a drink.

ST. CLARE. Not now; you must excuse me.

1ST CIT. Not drink with me? It is true, then, that you are now in sympathy with the temperance fanatics, and have forgot what is good for colds, and to keep the system regulated?

ST. CLARE. It is true that I have been accustomed to drink some, but I have resolved to refrain, and I shall endeavor to keep my resolution.

[2d *and* 3d Citizens *drunk and disputing.*

2D CIT. I say it was!

3D CIT. I say it was not! [*Strikes him.*

[*They fight, and* ST. CLARE, *in attempting to part them, is stabbed.*[29]

ST. CLARE. O murder! I am stabbed! I shall die—die, and leave my business unarranged: I promised Tom his liberty! [*He is carried away.*

[*Exeunt.*

SCENE XVI.

A Plantation on Red River.—Slaves' *Cabin.*—*Enter* EMELINE *and* CASSY.

EME. To be a slave—a slave to such a beast—to such a devil! O Cassy, I can't endure it! Can't we get away?

CAS. We might try; but, if we should be caught—

EME. What would he do, Cassy?

CAS. What would he not do? I have not told you yet that I have heard screams back at the quarters that almost make me afraid now to think of; and there is a tree not far away, burnt black, and the ground about it covered with ashes! No one would dare tell you what was done there; but you know how poor Tom has suffered—almost killed because he sung Christian hymns, and prayed, and because he would not practise flogging on me; and all this for nothing but to take the piety out of him, and teach him to be such kind of overseer as Sambo and Quimbo.

EME. Poor Tom! It is a wonder that he has so

nearly recovered from his wounds; and if we had not carried water to him, and taken good care of him, he would have died: yet that would have been better than to be a slave to such a master.

CAS. Something dreadful must happen to Tom yet; for I know he can't be broke in so that he will give up praying and go to flogging; I know he will never do that. Tom has known what it is to have kind masters.

EME. Yes; when he was up in old Kentuck, and took care of his master Shelby's farm, he had a better time.

CAS. I have heard him speak of it, but I have not heard him tell why he was sold, to be sent down here in this lower country.

EME. His master had to sell him and other of his slaves, to pay debts.

CAS. But if Shelby's slaves all worked as well as Tom, I don't see why his master need have been compelled to sell him.

EME. O Cassy, I have learned of Tom that wine has done all this! Shelby was a gentleman, but he drank, and made bad bargains, and expended too much of his money in festivities; therefore Tom was sold to a slave-dealer.

CAS. Yet he got into the hands of a good master

when St. Clare bought him; and if St. Clare had not been taken suddenly out of the world, Tom would not now be in the hands of Legree.

EME. Yes, St. Clare was a good master—was good to Tom—but he was not good to himself; for he got into the habit of frequenting the tavern, where he drank occasionally: and it was while trying to separate two drunken men fighting, that he was stabbed by one of them, and died before he could make out Tom's free papers; for he had promised Tom his liberty. Oh! liquor does the greatest mischief to masters; makes them insolvent, and makes them devils sometimes, when they drink enough of it. O what a devil it makes of Legree! He also gives drink to Sambo and Quimbo: no wonder they can do such floggings, and grin like devils all the time. Cassy, you know Massa Legree spends much time at the tavern over in town, and you know how he drinks and carouses; and I tell you that all his property—niggers, plantation, and all—will be sold sometime to pay his debts. This plantation is going to ruin now in his hands.

CAS. O Emeline, I see it is drink that causes our great troubles: drink makes masters squander the property they get by their slaves; drink makes them devils sometimes. Yet I drink; yes, Emeline, I drink brandy whenever I can get it. It makes me forget that I have been sold away from the husband that I loved and who loved me, and that I have got a master now who is a very devil!

EME. Mother used to tell me never to drink any of the bad liquors; she said it had been the cause of the most of her troubles.

CAS. I know it is a bad thing, yet I'd rather be drunk all the time while I am a slave to Legree—would n't you?

EME. O Cassy! let us runaway, and end our miseries some other way than by drinking brandy. Even if we should be caught, and flogged or burned to death, it would be better than to be a slave to a devil!

CAS. We will try to escape; and if we get away safely beyond his reach, then I will be happy, and drink no more.

EME. O Heaven help us! Let us prepare our bundles and go immediately. Let me direct, for I think I know the course best. [*Exeunt.*

SCENE XVII.

In a Bar-room.—Enter Landlord, Smollick, Jack, *and* Quimbo.

Land. [*Filling jugs.*] Then your master's gals Cassy and Emeline have really run away?

Quim. Yes, Mas'r,[30] run away, and we are going to have a hunt for them: the planters about are going to join us, and the brandy is for the company; so we will have a jolly time.

Land. If you catch them, what will you do to them?

Quim. Don't know: we will do what Mas'r Legree tells us; I reckon they will fare hard. Mas'r Legree wants your honor and Smollick to join in the hunt.

Land. Tell your master we will take pleasure in that.

Smol. Yes, we will, and he may expect us soon.

[*Exit* Quimbo, *with two jugs of brandy.*

Land. What a good supply of brandy he has got for the occasion! Legree is the right kind of a man, and it is a pleasure to assist him on such occasions.

SMOL. Yes, he is a real good fellow, and we will have a regular spree: he don't mind spending money for the good of himself and friends. We have had a great many jolly good sprees here at his expense, although he is like the devil sometimes when he has got a good quantity of brandy in him. I reckon he has got a good supply of that article to help us through the swamps, over logs, through bushes, over quagmires. Come, let us go: my appetite tells me it is time for the hunt to begin.

LAND. Come on. We will take our guns along.—Jack, attend the bar, and keep all things right.

[*Exeunt.*

SCENE XVIII.

A Plantation on Red River.—Enter LEGREE *and* QUIMBO.

LEG. We have hunted long enough in the swamps for the runaway gals without finding them. That cussed Tom is at the bottom of this affair—I know he is. Go, Quimbo, and bring him here quickly: he shall tell all he knows about it, though I have to roast him. [*Exit* QUIMBO.] That cussed Tom, ha! he was so mighty pious that he would n't whip the gal Cassy when I ordered him to do it—a queer beginning for a nigger that I thought to make an overseer of. And what pious excuses!—"Ain't used to flogging; never did, and can't do it no way." I wonder what he did up in old Kentuck when he was overseer there as he told me he had been? There is a smart chance of things for him to learn yet, and he shall learn them all, though his bones be broken in learning them. "Willing to do work, but not flogging." Ha! I'll let him know that flogging is work, when I tell him to do it. I reckon, though, that his piety is about gone now, after the flogging which I gave him, and which Sambo and Quimbo gave him when I gave him over to them to break him in. Sambo and Quimbo can do flogging—they like to do it—and to flog Tom is especial fun for them; for they know I purchased him for an overseer, and therefore they hate him. A slave tell me he don't think it right to do what I tell him! Ha! I'll see whether he will think it right to tell me where the gals Cassy and Emeline have gone. [*Drinks from his flask.*

Enter QUIMBO, *with* TOM.

Well, Tom, I've determined to kill you, unless you tell me where the runaway gals are: so speak quick!

UNCLE TOM. I don't know, mas'r.

LEG. Ye don't know, eh? Well, I'll make you know; so take that, and that!

[*Strikes him on the head with the butt-end of a loaded whip-stock.* TOM *staggers and falls.*

UNCLE TOM. O Lord, my heavenly Master, take my spirit home, where the wicked cease from troubling and the weary are at rest! [*Dies.*

LEG. More Bible, eh? but I reckon ye are done kicked the bucket now.—Well, I don't want pious niggers on my plantation. All *my* niggers have got to acknowledge *me* as their only master.—Take him away, Quimbo; and if he does not breathe again, put him into the ground. [*Exeunt.*

SCENE XIX.

A Forest in AMERICA.—*Enter* BEELZEBUB, *meeting* DIABOLOS, MAMMON, IMP, *and* BACCHO.

DIAB. Hail, great Beelzebub! I come again
And offer now more tidings of success.
BEEL. All hail, Diabolos! I wait to hear.
DIAB. You did advise, 't is done accordingly:—
Legree is victim of vile essences
Adulterated vilest, and the acts
Which I have instigated him to do
By such means, are already known afar,
I have no doubt. The wind sighs audibly,
And sympathy for those who felt his power
Begins sad movement!
BEEL. This I have observed
And know thy part exceedingly well done,
In causing such occurrence, and as much
As possible, that sympathy shall be
Compounded with the vilest essences
And thus occasion more advantages.

DIAB. I am not well assured how that may be;
For in the latitudes north of the line
That makes division, those who sympathize
Most with the slave, if I do not mistake,
Are generally those who do not give
Favor to prevalence of vilest drinks.
BEEL. To that consideration I accede,
Yet circumstances otherwhere are not
The same, especially in Albion;
For there we may commingle sympathy
With drinks, and loud will be the people's shouts
To swell the voice 'gainst slavery in the west;
Nor will they recognize themselves as slaves
More abject on their way down into hell!
And even here, as far as possible,
The question lying 'twixt the north and south
Shall be to all appearance paramount
To every other; so our wiles shall work;
And by the bottle we will do anon
Great injuries; and yet we will do these
In such a manner that they shall appear
To be sole consequence of slavery;
And we will then be able so to stir
The waters of the pool political,
As to divide the Union! then our sway
By vilest liquors will increase so vast

That ruin shall receive this nation—FALLEN!
For when this Union fails, ha! then fails all
Its harmony—its peace; and then will strife
Find brother watching brother far estranged,
Nor will he see whence comes the greatest harm
That can befall a soul immortal! Ha!
Then will succeed best opportunities
Of wiles, and triumph be anon complete;
For then will come on earth a darker age
Than any that has ever palled it yet!
Now let your way direct to Albion,
To mingle drink with sympathy for slaves!
Go forth, and do your mighty acts; for there
Great mischief waits your thither way in haste.

[*Exit* BEELZEBUB.

DIAB. Ha! what an instrument the bottle is,
We will divide the Union with the bottle.

MAM. I will do service there by mixing drinks,
And medicating them in various ways,
And so my fortunes vastly will increase.

IMP. I will get the medicines and do thee great assistance.

BAC. And I will make good use of the mixtures: I will have great revelings among the red-noses and beer-heads, and the very thinking of it excites me comfortably. Oftentimes I have had feasts, to which thousands gathered into one imbibing contiguity, and then the revelings and fightings that belonged to the occasion, were real!—not imaginary.[31] [*Exeunt.*

SCENE XX.

A Country in England.—*Enter* Diabolos *and* Mammon.

Diab. Now on the continent across the sea
Murmurs arise against oppression of
The Ethiop slave as instanced in the power
Legree did exercise at our control:—
Mammon, hast thou as yet arranged affairs
For the approaching opportunities.

Mam. I have, and shortly will proceed to work
Their full accomplishment.

Diab. What hast thou done?

Mam. I have given order for a million labels,
And sent Imp to bring hither articles
For great adulteration of the drinks
That bring me many fortunes.

Diab. Very well—
What are the labels for? what kind of labels?

Mam. Labels to make men's eyes so prominent

That jugs can be hung on them really—
Labels for bottles and of many kinds,
Which read "Uncle Tom Beer, Uncle Tom Gin,
Uncle Tom Wine, Uncle Tom Cogniac,
Uncle Tom Gullet-washer, Uncle Tom
Invigorator," and great many kinds.[32]

DIAB. No doubt thy profits will be very great.

MAM. O, certainly; for Uncle Tom, you know,
Was really a saint, and Englishmen,
Drinking the liquor in the labeled bottles,
Will think it fills them with divinity!

DIAB. Ha! well thou canst attend to these affairs,
And I will be among the multitudes,
At times convenient, gouging eyes, stabbing,
Shooting, and doing many spiteful tricks.
Meanwhile I will attend the workshops, where
I thrash the ragged urchins till they smell
Infernal power and answer with a yell.[33]

[*Exit* DIABOLOS.

MAM. 'Tis my desire that Imp make quick return
With medicines with which I doctor beer
And other liquors of vile quality,
And make them viler in a vast degree.
There are physicians that in studied practice
Cure some diseases by creating others
Of more malignant stamp, and such am I,

Well skilled in my profession. Now I see
That Imp has come with medicines for me.

Enter IMP.

IMP. Medicines not for thee, but for the beer.

MAM. O ho! it is all the same.

IMP. Have these medicines the proper smell?

MAM. They smell of the mineral, the vegetable,
And the animal kingdoms.

IMP. From those kingdoms I have brought them according to thy direction, thou notable doctor, thou skillful doctor.

MAM. Thou knowest well, I am a skillful doctor.

IMP. Ay, thou dost cure all diseases of beer and viler liquors, therefore I know, thou art a skillful doctor. I know the cause of the ailings of mankind, but the cause of the ailings of beer, I know little of.

MAM. Then tell of that only which thou knowest: What is the cause of men's ailings?

IMP. O, beer—beer of that special quality recovered from disease with these medicines by thy empiricism, destroys the nervous vitality that there be not enough strength in the system to oppose the intrusion of gouts, colics, cramps, gripings, rheumatisms, neuralgias, dyspepsias, apoplexies, and many others set down in the familiar nosology: it also fumes away the sensible of the mind and leaves there all the crude and the splenetic; but the cause of the indisposition of beer, tell me, Mammon, that verity may respond to my apprehension.

MAM. No mystery at all: a large quantity of beer made of little malt and hops, or strong beer mixed with water—that kind of beer which will not command sale for one diminutive piece of the red metal, is diseased.

IMP. If it would command ready sale, would it then be diseased?

MAM. O no—no!

IMP. Then the disease must be in the wills of the drinkers.

MAM. No; for if it were, recovery would come by medicating their wills, but I medicate the beer and so recover it from its indisposition for sale; therefore the disease is in the beer.

IMP. It must have many diseases to require such large variety of medicines as I have brought here at your direction.

MAM. It hath many, and each of such malignant character that it requires several qualities of medicine for its cure. Those diseases are all wants: one is the want of alcohol; another the want of bitterness; another the want of pungency; another the want of muddiness; another the want of age; another the want of astringency; another the want of froth: I cure them all.

IMP. Then thou art a cure-all, a panacea. O Panacea! I thought that the beer had only one disease, — the want of sale.

MAM. Ay, that is the stage to which all the others tend and prove mortal, unless these remedies be applied: What hast thou here?

IMP. All that thou didst tell me to bring: this is treacle; this is alum; this is coriander; this is caraway; this is henbane; this is vitriol; this is St. Ignatius bean; this is opium; this is cocculus indicus, this is Bohemia rosemary; this is wormwood; this is aloes; this is quassia; this is gentian; this is fish; this is clam-shell: this is potash; this is lime.

MAM. All proper medicines for the recovery of beer, but the medicines for the good of brandy, and gin, and rum, and whisky; hast thou brought the full quantity?

IMP. Ay, here is oil of vitriol; oil of cassia; oil of turpentine; oil of caraways; oil of juniper; oil of almonds; sulphuric ether; extract of capsicums; extract of orris root; extract of Angelica root; water; sugar; saffron; mace; terra japonica; nitre; aqua ammonia.

MAM. A proper collection, and very good for the liquors.

IMP. And very good-bad for the drinkers, which is seen in the quicker effect of making the eyes water, and the firing up of their noses, and the causing of the tottering in their locomotions.

MAM. Well, it is all in aid of our government in the world. Ha! here comes Baccho with an anxious look which, I have no doubt, has regard for the good-vile juices.

Enter BACCHO.

BAC. Ho, for more of the medicated and the mixed liquors!

MAM. Thy desires are of such a quality that I regard them with great favor; yet is not this country full of liquors? Really, it is my interest to have plentiful supply for all contingencies.

BAC. But see what a commotion is now making noise through all this island; and it is the commotions that in this country especially, bring liquor in very great requisition. Uncle Tom, who was a saint and hated the good-vile drinks,[34] and who lived across the big waters when he lived, and who was killed by Legree when he died, is wept for here with a kind of sympathy that has no sympathy with the urchin starvelings of the workshops on this big island, which ought to be surrounded by a great sea of real liquor instead of the brine, which is not good for drinking at all: And to-night Uncle Tom is to be represented at the theatre, and I shall be among the audience making applause; and I shall give out such an odor of beer and stronger liquors, which being smelt, the auditors will quickly forget that they have any troubles, such as poverty from the intoxicating liquors, the loss of friends from the intoxicating liquors, and the many that be hanged for what they did by the influence of the intoxicating liquors, and the many that be starving because of the intoxicating liquors; and when they shall have forgotten all this, they will shed tears, like crocodiles, over the fate of Uncle Tom, who became a victim of our victim across the waters!

MAM. O, that be very well, Baccho! and we are making great preparation for medicating and mixing the liquors; and thou hast come at fit time to render great assistance by smelling and tasting them, by which means, we can have true guide to bring them quickly to their full perfection. Come, we will proceed to the operation in my laboratory. Very many liquors, which shall have proper age and all other good qualities, shall be prepared for to-night's drinking. [*Exeunt.*

SCENE XXI.

A Gin-shop in LONDON,[35]—Landlord *waiting on* Customers.—*Enter a* Citizen.

CIT. [*Looking at the bottles in the bar.*] *H*uncle Tom beer, eh? *H*uncle Tom brandy, eh? *H*uncle Tom gin, eh?

LAND. Yes, *h*and the best kind of drinks—no mistake.

CIT. Well, I'll take some of the *H*uncle Tom gin. It must be good, although *h*it 'as not 'ad time to *h*acquire the good quality of *h*age; for *h*it is something new, of course.

LAND. No, you mistake: I got *h*it direct from Mr. Mammon's laboratory, where *h*it 'as been *h*undergoing the process of *h*acquiring *h*age *h*ever since *H*uncle Tom was born.

CIT. Ah! 'as *h*it? Well, 'ere's to the repose of *H*uncle Tom, and the downfall of American slavery!

[*Drinks.*

LAND. American slavery *h*is a dreadful thing: 'ow poor *H*uncle Tom suffered *h*at the 'ands of 'is cruel master!

CIT. Cruel, cruel!—But what *h*is that box for?

LAND. Read the label, *h*and you will see: you *h*are a generous man.

CIT. [*Reads.*] *This box is to receive penny contributions to put down slavery in the United States. It is hoped this worthy object will enlist the co-operation of all.* Well, I'll put in a penny; for I 'ave *h*as much sympathy for the poor slave *h*as my *h*appetite 'as for beer, gin, brandy, or whisky. *H*it *h*is a pity there *h*is so much suffering *h*in the world.

LAND. A great pity; but *h*if *h*our greatest grandmother *H*eve 'ad not *h*eaten a forbidden *h*apple, the world now would *h*all be 'appy, *h*and there would be no slaves *h*in America, where they *h*are most starved, scarcely clothed, worked to death, *h*and then flogged *h*entirely to death! Oh, *h*it *h*is 'orrible—'orrible!

CIT. *H*uncle Tom is to be represented *h*in a play *h*at the Liquor-'all Theatre to-night, and *h*it will be a first-rate performance, of course.

LAND. Per'aps: *h*are you going to *h*attend?

CIT. Yes, if I 'ave money *h*enough. Let me see: I 'ave got just a shilling; that will take me *h*in.—'Eigh-'o! 'urra for *H*uncle Tom! This shilling, which my wife 'id away, comes 'andy now. What business 'ad she to 'ide money from me? *H*am I not lord of my wife? *H*are not the men lord of the women? 'As not a man the right to take care of *h*all the money *h*after they *h*are united *h*in matrimony?

LAND. Of course 'e 'as.

CIT. Of course 'e 'as! *H*are you going to the theatre, landlord?

LAND. No, I can not go; I 'ave to remain 'ere to *h*attend to the wants of my customers; it will not do to neglect them: these *H*uncle Tom drinks *h*are *h*in great demand.

CIT. Success to the drinks, *h*and joy to the drinkers! I'm for the theatre. 'Urra for *H*uncle Tom!

[*Exit* Citizen.

LAND. I 'ave no doubt that the play of *H*uncle Tom *h*at Liquor-'all, will be a good one; but, *h*after *h*all, 'e might *h*as well 'ave remained 'ere *h*and spent 'is money for *H*uncle Tom drinks. Really, 'e *h*ought to know that the *h*administering to the *h*appetite *h*is the *h*only way to *h*obtain real *h*enjoyment; for *h*in that way *h*all 'is cares *h*and troubles *h*in this life would be banished, *h*and the *h*annoyances by the *h*importunities which I know 'e is *h*often subjected to from the wants of 'is wife *h*and children would not *h*affect 'im *h*any *h*at *h*all! Really, the people *h*ought to spend *h*all their money *h*at my bar: 'ere's where they can get the worth of their money!

Enter a Woman.

'Ere again, eh? Well, what d'ye want? 'Aven't I told you not to come 'ere *h*any more?—So get *h*away from 'ere!

WOMAN. Please, sir, I wish to know *h*if my 'usband 'as been 'ere.

LAND. Well, 'e 'as, *h*and 'e 'as gone *h*away again. So, go *h*away, woman!

WOMAN. Please, sir, where 'as 'e gone?

LAND. I know not, *h*and I care not; nor will I care where you go—but begone!

WOMAN. [*Going.*] O I wish 'e was *h*at 'ome! Please, landlord, don't sell my 'usband *h*any more liquor!

LAND. That's what I *h*expected. No more of your *h*importunities: I've been *h*annoyed enough with them! My liquors are my property, *h*and I'll do what I choose with them, without *h*asking the *h*advice of a woman. We *h*all 'ave to take the world *h*as *h*it 'appens—so go *h*away, woman!

[*The* Woman *goes to her home; and when the bell tolls the midnight hour, her* Husband *is brought to her* DEAD, *having been killed in a drunken fight! The* Murderer, *of course, is to be hanged.*

SCENE XXII.

A Northern City.— Street before the Notional Theatre.—People *entering the Theatre.—Enter the Street, two* Southerners.—*Music within.*

1st South. That is good music. This is a theatre: let us go in and see the play.

2d South. It is the Notional Theatre, and, for special reasons, I will not patronize it. However, let us see what the play is. [*Reads the bill.*] "Notional Theatre. Uncle Tom's Cabin every Night!—Unparalleled Success of this Great Moral Drama!"

1st South. Why, the play must be about Uncle Tom, who was killed by his cruel master, Legree. It is unfortunate that such a person should ever own a slave.

2d South. It is; but our system allows it.

1st South. But there are laws that protect the slave from cruelty.

2d South. True; yet they give no protection when they are not enforced.

1st South. Public sentiment against the abuse of slaves is their great protection.

2d South. It did not protect Uncle Tom.

1st South. But I have learned that Legree's plantation and slaves have been sold, and that he has left the country. Did not public sentiment compel him to do so?

2d South. No: the same circumstance that had taken the property from its former proprietor, took it also from Legree. Its former owner had become insolvent from the effects of intemperance, and the property was sold cheap at sheriff's sale, and Legree became the purchaser. But the tavern in the town near by, is the legendary of sad reverses. Legree was fond of the intoxicating beverages, and, in no mysterious way, his property went from his hands, and he himself has gone—I know not where.

1st South. Legree is an unfortunate—a wretched man.

2d South. He is, indeed. I have learned, from one more familiar with him, that there were times when a singular feeling would possess him, and he would exclaim: "O Celestra!—Is it possible?—The Notional Theatre!—That fatal drink!" I believe, if we were to know more concerning him, we would be more inclined to pity than to blame; and it is possible that the bar-room in this very theatre, may have had much to do with his first step to ruin.—The crowd has gone in. Let us see what these pictures are. [*Advancing into the vestibule, and observing pictures hanging on the wall.*] This picture seems to represent Mr. Shelby and Haley drinking and making terms about the sale of Uncle Tom. The changes of Uncle Tom's fortune are in those glasses of wine; for it was this kind of indulgence which so controlled Mr. Shelby's affairs that he was obliged to sell his slaves! Let us depart: we have got too near the liquid poison within; for I smell its offensive odor! I am already sick with a surfeit of curiosity, and have no desire to enter.

1ST SOUTH. Well, if this is a place, where, for money, they make characters like Legree—make men beasts; and then, for money, exhibit their beastly actions as curiosities! I also have no desire to enter. [*Exeunt.*

TICKET-SELLER. [*Putting his head through the ticket-door and thinking aloud.*] Southern gentlemen, eh? Wal, I don't "keer" whar' a man comes from; if he only pays his quarter he can go in, and if he don't, why, he can walk away; but, after all, I wish they had paid their quarters and gone in; for, really, this is the place where they can get the worth of their money, especially in the play of Uncle Tom, where they can see plantation manners—see themselves as others see 'em.—But there comes a hard-looking customer if he be a customer at all;—no matter—if he has got a quarter he can see great sights inside.

Enter SIMON LEGREE *intoxicated.*

LEG. What bill is this, eh? [*Reads*] "NOTIONAL THEATRE. UNCLE TOM'S CABIN EVERY NIGHT! UNPARALLELED SUCCESS OF THIS GREAT MORAL DRAMA"! Why, this is the Notional Theatre. I think I 've been here before.—Should n't wonder if I have; I was here with Malverton—took a drink—and—O Celestra!—but that's past!—I will not think of her. Uncle Tom's Cabin must be a real curiosity; for I burnt it up before I left the plantation, and it must have come up here on the principle that the resurrection will be got up on: really, I would like to see the ghost of Tom's cabin; I could tell if it be genuine; for I know every feature of it,—I know how all the logs looked,—where every knot was and every piece of bark; I would not be afeard of it either; I ain't afeard of anything; I would n't be afeard if Tom himself should appear and occupy it; no, not I. Let me see; I have a quarter left, and enough besides to pay for a drink. I must see the curiosities. [*Ad-*

vances into the vestibule.] But what pict'res are these? [*Reads*] "HALEY MAKING TERMS WITH SHELBY FOR SLAVES." Why, that must be the Shelby of old Kentuck'—Tom's former master that I heard him tell of. Well, I don't care anything about Shelby, nor Haley, but I'd like to have a good swig of that liquor they ar' drinkin'. The very pict're of those bottles and glasses, makes my mouth water for liquor—some real rum, or gin, or whisky, or cogniac; but I'll have to wait till I get inside, I reckon: But what kind of a picture is this? [*Observing a picture of Uncle Tom being whipped, and reads*] "UNCLE TOM WITH ANOTHER MASTER." Putting the whip on 'im, eh? "Wal," that looks really nat'ral. That's the way to make a nigger dance. [*Hops up.*] Go it, Tom, if that's you; and I believe it is; for it looks just like you,—a real pious nigger: I feel as if I should like to have hold of that whip: I'm used to that kind of business: I could make the very pict're of Tom hop right up! [*Hops up*]—but—but—I'm out of that business now. My plantation is gone, and niggers too! I must see the play; for it will be amusement: may be they'll want some applause made, and if they do, I can do that just as easy as blowing on a whistle after I have oiled my blower with a little rum or gin, or whisky, or brandy.—I say, Mr. [*to the*

Ticket Agent] how much will I have to pay to go in and see the performance?

T. Agent. You can go in for a quarter.

Leg. "Wal," here 't is; it is the last quarter I've got, but I've got enough left to buy a drink or two of the good O-be-joyful, at the bar within: I am glad you have such good accommodations.

[*Pays his quarter and goes in.*

SCENE XXIII.

On a Steamboat descending the Ohio River.—Enter a Southerner *and a* Northerner.

South. This is delightful view presented here,
Of the Ohio river and its shores.

North. It is.

South. The scenery upon each marge,
Especially, is very beautiful;
Those wide-branched sycamores and stately elms,
With foliage like to the emerald,
Are very pleasing to the view.

North. They are,
And must delight they eye of every one.

South. And if insatiate thence the vision turn

Deflecting glance into the lucid stream,
The imaged arbors perfectly appear,
Inverted, yet as grand as beautiful.
NORTH. There is much here presented to the view
That challenges affection of the eyes,
Which are indeed the servitors of mind.
The scenes that lie surrounding I admire,
Although not admirable equally,
To me, appear the separated shores.
SOUTH. But I can not observe the difference,
If there be any real difference,
In nature's handy-work upon the shores,
Between which lies this river's coursing way:
Each side possesses varied scenery,
Of cliffs, of hills, of plains, of fields, of woods;
All admirable in variety.
NORTH. All that is admirable I admire
In works of nature and of art, as far
As nature may, and art—themselves alone,
Resolve in the sublimer faculties;—
All this itself is pleasing to the eye,—
Itself is gratifying to the mind;
Yet there may be what of itself is fair,
Connected with associations, such,
That when the eye beholds, the mind grows sick,
And then the scene grows painful to the eye,

Which turns to be delightful otherwhere ;
So when I look upon the southern shore
Of the Ohio river, I grow sick
From the associations that arise
And fill my mind with painful contemplations ;
Therefore I rather turn my eyes away
From cliffs, and hills, and plains, and fields, and woods,
Which, on the shore that lies upon the south,
Are but the symbols in mnemonic art,
Presenting all the evil of the land,
Which evil has such vasty magnitude,
The Union is all blighted with its curse.

South. I must confess that I am not aware
To what you now allude, since, very oft,
Opinions are conflicting ; what to one,
Presents appearance very hideous,
Another looks on with indifference,
Yet shrinks aghast at what the former sees,
Mild and most specious in comparison :
And yet I think you may allude, perhaps,
To slavery, since what to me appears
An evil to be deprecated more
Is not here limited by parallel,
Nor any marge of any watery way.

North. I do allude to human slavery
For nothing else on earth is like to it,

Since of all evils, this presents the sum.
SOUTH. Sir, sir? ——
NORTH. A man made in the image of his God,
Must toil and sweat beneath the tyrant's lash,
That tyranny may lie on beds of ease!
What can afflict the contemplation more?
SOUTH. O, I can tell you! It is painful more
To see that image which is likest God's,
Struck down in everlasting ruins, that
The beasts can even gaze upon his fall,
Yet none can comprehend how low his fall!
O, sir! the evils of intemperance
O'er all this land, are spread in broad extent—
Dark is the curse and dire the misery
That follow on its desolating way!
NORTH. Yet it is voluntary on man's part,
If he degrade himself through appetite;
But 't is not, in regard to slavery—
One can not choose, and by that choice be free,
When power sways over him its mastery.
SOUTH. Though he can not, the will is not enslaved,
As in the case of appetite depraved,
Which is the greater bondage on the world,
Because thereby man's normal being yields
And is struck down into the deepest ruin!
My home is in the south, and yet I think

I have not learned unjust comparison.
  NORTH. I think you have; Look on the sunny
      south;
Behold the Ethiop blood and Anglican,
In concourse through the veins of servitude!
Say, who are they in bondage, not allowed
To learn of Heaven or hell except by proxy!—
Bought,—sold—made meanest chattels of!
Oppressors of the sunny south, these are—
Your sons and your daughters!—Think of it.
Th' day blushes; the night blackens over the
Enormities of your iniquities!
  SOUTH. Sir, sir,——
  NORTH. Receive it as you may; 'tis true.
  SOUTH. O who am I to listen, and not strike
A blow at once to punish insolence!
Am I coward?—am I not a coward?
You would appear a brave man: is it brave
To utter such uncharitable speech,
Presuming on defying attitude?
  NORTH. Whatever you may call it, let it pass:
I do not fear whatever you may do.
  SOUTH. Indeed! I hope it is not your design
To tempt me to do something I ought not,
And after, would be very sorry for,
When high-wrought passion be allayed again.

NORTH. I tempt no man; I only speak the truth.
Do what you may, I fear no southerner.

SOUTH. And must I bear all this? No: I will strike
And punish insolence, though afterward,
It should be more occasion for regret,
Than any other act of all my life.

[*Advances with a stiletto drawn from his cane: Northerner draws a pistol and retreats.*

NORTH. Hold! hold! I say, or I will blow you through!

SOUTH. No — no — I will not strike; for this is not
The virtue of a man, — this drunkards do
When they are wrought with the distempered draughts!

NORTH. I see it is this weapon that you fear.

SOUTH. I fear your weapon not; I fear myself.
It follows not essentially that I
Should be, like many of my countrymen,
Excited easily to fatal strife.
Nay: reason holds me back; it stays my hand;
For I have somewhat seen the world's wide ways
Whence many mischiefs rise, and I confess,
I rather judge you honest in your thoughts,
And let it pass as wisdom would advise.

NORTH. My thoughts are honest thoughts and true as honest.

SOUTH. I do not question it: I know that wrong
Exists in great degree in latitudes
Where instituted service bears its chains.

NORTH. A good confession; very good confession:
Whoever rather will confess a wrong
Than hide it, is deserving of respect,
And I am glad to hear you thus confess.
I could not dwell where slavery exists:
I rather be removed from all its curse
And scenes of horror, to some other clime
Where man's own offspring are not made his slaves,
To toil per-force and do his drudgery;
Where no Legrees and Lokers torture them,
And bring them victims to the gates of death.

SOUTH. Yet where is there a country free from wrongs.

NORTH. The northern part of these United States
Is free from wrongs like these.

SOUTH. O, is it so?
I know that in the country where I live,
Man is not all divine, nor half divine;
For frailty is the large inheritance
Of mortals there, however different
It may be in the country that you speak of;

For farther in the northern latitudes,
The composition of mankind is such,
That the intoxicating beverage,
Inflames the passions and depraves the thoughts
And the affections, so the consequence
Which makes the day blush and which blackens night,
Is that the master's sons and daughters are,
In many cases, illegitimate—
And born to the inheritance of chains!
There, poisonous potions are not good for man;
They drink the beverage and so become
Legrees and Lokers, and their dreadful acts
Are heralded abroad the wide, wide world.
NORTH. It matters not what causes evils deeds;
Bad acts are bad, whatever be the cause.
SOUTH. Banish the cause, the deeds will disappear,
Pray, tell me, sir, if in the northern states,
Men are so constituted that vile drink
Will harm them not?—say, are they proof against
The poisons of th' intoxicating cup,
So that thereby their passions may not task
All guilty consequence to bring reproach?
NORTH. Well, whether they be poison proof or not,
I need not intimate;—they have no slaves.
SOUTH. Yet that which doth degrade men lower than slaves,

Or even beasts, they have abundance of;
And that they give to men; nay, sell to men:
Ay, sell to us, remote the burning zone
Less far than this cold line. We drink the fire,
And then our acts be such that, judging us,
You think we scarce deserve the name of men.

NORTH. Your acts be wholly your own acts, not ours;
And yet you seek to implicate the north
In cruelties upon the Ethiop slave!
Is it not ever so with guiltiness?
Guilt ever seeks to hide its hideous shape,
By turning gaze upon some imperfection
In the accusing spirit.

SOUTH. Doth it so?
Whatever evil there be in the land
Where slaves toil, I would not attempt to hide.
But has the north not done them any wrong?
And if they have, may I not speak of it,
If I have any feeling for the wronged?—
And doth not this inquiry answer you?
But if it answer not, I'll answer, then,
"Guilt ever seeks to hide its hideous shape
By turning gaze upon some imperfection
In the accusing spirit."

NORTH. We need not

Debate unprofitably.

SOUTH. It may be
Not all unprofitable. If you please
Look yonder; can you tell what craft that is
We are approaching?

NORTH. Yes, it is a flat-boat.

SOUTH. You see those barrels on it, do you not?

NORTH. I do.

SOUTH. That humble boat, too, has a name.

NORTH. It has a name; for I can plainly see,
It is the "Whisky-dealer of Ohio."

Enter a Flat-boat loaded with whisky. The Steamboat, halting to set a passenger ashore, remains some little time in talking distance from the Flat-boat.

BOATMEN. [*Singing.*]

"Heigh-o, the boatmen row,
'Way down the river on the O-hi-o;
Heigh-o, the boatmen row,
'Way down the river on the O-hi-o;
Boatmen dance, boatmen sing,
Boatmen up to anything;
Boatmen dance, boatmen sing,
Boatmen up to anything."

SOUTH. Now I will speak with them, though they should think
I am impertinent when I shall ask

How far they go, and what they have aboard?
Halloo—the boat.
BOAT. Halloo, yourself, I say;—
Are you going to run all night?
SOUTH. How far do you go down the river, sir?
BOAT. [*Singing.*] O, way down the O-hi-o,
Then down the Mis-sis-sip-pi-o.
SOUTH. Excuse me, sir, what have you got aboard?
BOAT. O, we have got a jolly crew aboard!
And more than that, we've got a load of whisky.
SOUTH. I must not question it, but what, indeed
Is your *boat* loaded with?
BOAT. Whisky, I say.
SOUTH. I beg your pardon, now I understand
It is your boat thus loaded, not yourselves;
But tell me, pray, what is your whisky good for?
BOAT. O, it is good—'tis good—why, it is good
To drown cares, quench fears, and make men brave.
SOUTH. Does it drown cares? It brings them on in trains
Unceasing till the grave devours them all,—
All that are mortal;—some of them may live
Still on, and fill eternity with wo!
Does it quench fear? It rather makes men blind
To every danger, and step o'er the mark
Discretion lays betwixt the good and ill.

Ah! does it make men brave? It makes them rash,
And with temerity they rush on death!
Let him, and him alone, be counted brave
Who can withstand temptation's hard assaults
And 'gainst the evil passions in his breast
Wage a successful war;—but I would not
Give you unpleasant feelings;—if I do,
It gives me also pain, but I must speak
As I think may be service to mankind;
For I desire the greatest good of all.

1ST BOAT. O, no offence whatever, sir, and if
You judge our article of trade not good
For all the things that I have mentioned, then,
I'll tell you what 'tis good for;—It is good
To make Legrees of and Tom Lokers of!

ALL THE BOATMEN. [*Rowing and Singing.*]

"Heigh-o, the boatmen row
'Way down the river on the O-hi-o;
Heigh-o, the boatmen row
'Way down the river on the O-hi-o;
Boatmen dance,"——

[*The Flat-boat moves away.*

SOUTH. *To make Legrees of and Tom Lokers of!*—
But the Legrees and Lokers have not all
Their dwelling in the south; for well I know

I'll tell you what 't is good for; — It is good
To make Legrees of and Tom Lokers of!

PAGE 292.

That there are such inhabiting the north,
Which place my traverse way hath many times
Brought me along. On such occasion once,
When I was powerless to interfere,
I saw two men in furious combat strive,
Who were in state of partial drunkenness;
Each struggled hard to ward the other's blow
And thrust his weapon with a fatal aim!
I heard a cry!—I saw the champion
Rise from his foe, with the stiletto, true
To its sad purpose, quivering in his heart!
Then on the body sat the murderer,—
The severed head of his antagonist,
With blood-stained fingers twisted in its hair,
Dripped sanguinary drops while demon-like
He whirled it round, and swung it to and fro;
And a triumphant smile played on his lips,—
Smile which had wandered from infernal depths;
Then uttered horrid imprecations on
His victim, quite too awful to repeat,—
Prayed that his soul might find all else but rest,
And in a frenzy far too deep for earth
He muttered o'er and o'er his hellish prayer!

NORTH. But northern men do not alone afford
Means of intoxication to the south;
Yet I allow that gold hath tempted them

To furnish much infernal beverage,
Which I do wish were banished from the world,
Because the cup is full of cruelties,
Almost beyond all human utterance!

SOUTH. The tongue that tells its cruelties, should be
All lightning that the voice should falter not!
The ear that hears them, lest it afterward
Forget all sound, should be so far removed
That it could not distinguish if it be
The lightning's answer or the voice of winds,
Or rushing waters, or the din of war!
The pen that writes them, should be flint, and fire,
And steel, in order to endure the task!
The eyes that look upon them, should be all
Of stone, and dull as night, lest they should weep,
A flood of tears and drown the world again!
You say you wish it banished from the world.
You do wish so? Here is my hand —my heart—
No doubt we understand each other well—
And argument should have its period.

NORTH. My heart responds, and we will yet be friends:
On temperance our Liberty depends;
United, we will banish as a foe,
The poison-cup, which is a cup of wo. —

SOUTH. Which would usurp supremacy entire
And burn mankind with its consuming fire.

[*The boat moves away.*

SCENE XXIV.

A Forest in AMERICA.—*Enter* LUCIFER *and* BEELZEBUB.

BEEL. O Lucifer, thou hast observed how well
The powers at my command have followed out
The scheme which made such victim of Legree
As made the angels weep; yet while the acts
Which we have done, are sounded o'er the land
In solemn cadences, see what advance
Supernal powers have made against vile drinks.

LUC. I know how great the influence of all
Associations working now combined,
Their vast attempts; and yet this follows not
From the divisional disturbance, no;
For there is no relationship to cause
The like dependency, therefore we need
Chiefly do this—pursue the policy
Which makes Legree our victim,—with vile drinks
Perform innumerable acts, which they,

Who sympathize with suffering, will deem
Abomination; yet conceal the cause
So that reacting effort operate
Upon effects alone; and by such means
We yet will counteract opposing power;
For violence upon the government
Of these United States, shall by the drink,
Be carried to its utmost—so shall fall
This Union, and for ever then will be
Distracting feuds while fullest liberty
Shall follow to the instruments of ill—
And even now in Kansas have we not
Established rule? for there the fiery essence
Blasts the immortal man!

BEEL. Ay, very true—
That country is on *our* side of the line
Already; for the deeply-burning liquids
There serve our will!

LUC. Arise now, fallen spirits;
And soon this Union shall be victimized
And not this Union only, but the world!

BEEL. It shall be;—there is power enough in lies
To fill this world with sighs and miseries! [*Exeunt.*

SCENE XXV.

Within a Hospital—LEGREE *on a Bed.*—Attendants.

LEG. What place is this? Why are these devils here?
Away! away! for this place is not hell!
Now vipers cling to me! O, take them off!
Now they are crawling over me! Take off
These snakes—they hiss at me! O, horrible!
Protect me from these dread pursuing fiends
That multiply around me with their torments!
Now flames dance round—now darkness strikes me blind.
Now frightful beings indescribable
Gaze on me hideous! I shut my eyes
To see them not, and yet I see them still!
Do ye not see them, and do ye not hear them?
Now I am falling! falling!—where am I?
Oh! what a vast and absolute abyss!
Off, Demons! Oh! is there no one who will
Deliver me from terrors? O God!—but

There is no God who will deliver me;—
Celestra, O, Celestra, where are you—
You who would never leave me comfortless
While you were on earth to comfort me—
Where are you now? Come, save me from these
fiends!
These fiery dragons!—But she is in heaven:
'T is well,—but I am going into hell!
Take off these snakes! Take off their icy coils!
They glare at me with dreadful eyes of fire!
I'll take them off;—but now I can not feel
My body with my hands.[36] Where am I now?
I have no body sensible to touch!
My spirit disembodied falls in torments!
Celestra, save me, save me, O Celestra!— [*Dies.*

END OF PART III.

NOTES TO THE DRAMA OF EARTH.

Note 1.—*Page* 28.

For here the habitation is, of man—
The highest of intelligences that
Inhabit any orb.

We have reason to believe that most of the planets are inhabited by intelligent beings, but of what characters, and what degrees of intelligence, we can not resolve; and, for the purposes of this drama, it may be of little consequence if it should be *discovered* that I have erred in representing the primitive inhabitants of this earth as beings intellectually superior to those who may inhabit other planets.

Note 2.—*Page* 38.

Upon the next day, in the evening.

Although *forenoon* and *afternoon* are used respectively for *morning* and *evening*, yet the latter have also been in use from ancient time, and are now generally used in the southern states.

NOTE 3.—*Page* 46.

His labor here among these fruitful trees.

MAN was placed in the Garden of Eden to dress it and keep it. Of course we are to understand that this was *labor*, which, in a moderate degree, is not a curse. If mankind were now in their normal state, all who are neither too old nor too young, would be in the condition to labor, and would have intelligence so that little, very little of their labor would prove without effect or be lost, and therefore all could have the proper luxuries of life by means of that amount of labor which is—not a curse—but a blessing.

NOTE 4.—*Page* 50.

Enter LUCIFER *in the shape of an Orang-Outang.*

I KNOW not that it is of any importance whether the form which Satan assumed when he beguiled the first human pair, was, or was not, that of a *serpent.* In this drama I have chosen to represent it as one of the simia genus; and however much it may be supposed to be the subject of exceptions, is also of little account; and whether either the literal, or the allegorical interpretation of the Mosiac account of the fall of man, be the correct one instead of the other, it can not affect the truth that evil is in the world, and that it is the same, by whatever agent it may have been caused. However, for the benefit of those who may read this volume, and be curious to learn what *reasons* there may be for believing that the animal which the tempter possessed on that occasion, may have been as well one of the simia tribe, as a serpent,—and who may not otherwise have convenient access to those *reasons*—I submit the following exegesis of the scriptural reference to the same, as given by Dr. Adam Clarke, whose reputation of being learned in the languages, may entitle it to favorable consideration.

"We have here [Gen. chap. iii.] one of the most difficult, as well as the most important narratives in the whole book of God. The last chapter ended with a short, but striking account of the perfection and felicity of the first human beings, and this opens with an account of their transgression, degradation, and ruin. That man is in a fallen state, the history of the world, with that of the life and miseries of every human being, establish beyond successful contradiction. But *how*, and by what agency, was this brought about? Here is a great mystery; and I may appeal to all persons who have read the various comments that have been written on the Mosaic account, whether they have ever yet been satisfied on this part of the subject, though convinced of the fact itself. Who was the serpent? Of what kind, in what way did he seduce the first happy pair? These are questions which *remain yet to be answered.* The whole account is either a simple narration of facts, or it is an allegory. If it be a historical relation, its literal meaning should be sought out; if it be an allegory, no attempt should be made to explain it, as it would require a direct revelation to ascertain the sense in which it should be understood; for fanciful illustrations are endless. Believing it to be a simple relation of facts capable of a satisfactory explanation, I shall take it up on this ground, and by a careful examination of the original text, endeavor to fix the meaning and show the propriety and consistency of the Mosaic account of the Fall of Man. The chief difficulty in the account is found in the question: Who was the agent employed in the seduction of our first parents?

"The word in the text, which we, following the Septuagint, translate serpent, is נחש *nachash*, and according to *Buxtorf* and others, has *three* meanings in scripture. 1. It signifies to *view* or *observe attentively*, to *divine* or *use enchantments*, because in them the augurs *viewed attentively* the *flight* of *birds*, the *entrails* of *beasts*, the *course* of the *clouds*, etc., and under this head it signifies to *acquire knowledge by experience*. 2. It signifies *brass*, *brazen*, and is translated in our Bible, not only *brass*, but *chains*, *fetters*, *fetters* of *brass*, and in several places *steel*: see 2 Sam. xxii. 35; Job xx. 24; Psal. xviii. 34; and in one place, at least, *filthiness* or *fornication*; Ezekiel, xvi. 36. 3. It signifies a *serpent*, but of what kind is not determined. In Job xxvi. 13, it seems to mean the *whale* or *hippopotamus*. *By his spirit he hath garnished the heavens; his hand hath formed the crooked serpent*, נחש ברח *nachash bariach; as* ברח *barach* signifies to *pass on* or *pass through*, and בריח *beriach* is used for a bar of a gate or door *that passed through rings*, etc., the idea of *straightness* rather than *crookedness*, should be attached to it here; and it is likely that the *hippopotamus* or *sea-horse* is intended by it. In Eccles x. 11, the creature called *nachash* of whatever sort, is compared to the *babbler*. *Surely the serpent* (נחש *nachash*), *will bite without enchantment; and a babbler is no better.*

"In Isai. xxvii. 1, the crocodile or alligator seems particularly meant by the original. *In that day the Lord shall punish leviathan, the piercing serpent,* etc. And in Isai. lxv. 25, the same creature is meant as in Gen. iii. 1, for in the words: *And dust shall be the serpent's meat,* there is an evident allusion to the text of Moses. In Amos, ix. 3, the crocodile is evidently intended. *Though they be hid in the bottom of the sea, thence will I command the serpent* (הנחש *hannachash*), *and he shall bite them.* No person can suppose that any of the *snake* or *serpent* kind can be intended here; and we see from the various acceptations of the word, and the different senses which it bears in various places in the sacred writings, that it appears to be a sort of *general term* confined to no one sense. Hence it will be necessary to examine the root accurately, to see if its ideal meaning will enable us to ascertain the animal intended in the text. We have already seen that נחש *nachash* signifies to *view attentively,* to *acquire knowledge,* or *experience by attentive observation;* so נחשתי *nichashti* (Gen. xxx. 27), *I have learned by experience;* and this seems to be its most general meaning in the Bible. The original word is, by the Septuagint, translated οφις, a *serpent,* not because this was its *fixed* determinate meaning in the sacred writings, but because it was the best that occurred to the translators; and they do not seem to have given themselves much trouble to understand the meaning of the original; for they have rendered the word as variously as our translators have done; or rather our translators have followed *them,* as they give nearly the same significations found in the Septuagint; hence we find that οφις is as frequently used by them as *serpent,* its supposed literal meaning as used in our version. And the New Testament writers who seldom quote the Old Testament, *but from the Septuagint translation*, and do not often *change* a word in their quotations, copy this version in the use of this word. From the Septuagint, therefore, we can expect no light, nor indeed from any other of the ancient versions, which are all *subsequent* to the Septuagint, and some of them actually made from it. In all this uncertainty, it is natural for a serious inquirer after truth, to look *everywhere* for information. And in such an inquiry, the Arabic may be expected to afford some help, from its great similarity to the Hebrew. A root in this language, very similar to that in the text, seems to cast considerable light on the subject : خنس *chanas*, or *khanasa*, signifies *he departed, drew off, lay hid, seduced, slunk away;* from this root come اخنس *akhnas*, خنسا *khanasa*, and خنوس *khanoos*, which all signify an *ape*, or *satyrus*, or any creature of the *simia* or ape genus.

"It is very remarkable also that from the same root comes خناس *khanas*, the *devil*, which appellative he bears from that meaning of خنس *khanasa*, *he drew off, seduced*, etc., because he *draws* men *off* from righteousness, *seduces* them from their obedience to God, etc. Is it not strange that the *devil* and the ape should have the same name, derived from the same root, and that root so very similar to the word in the text? But let us return and consider what is said of the creature in question. *Now the nachash was more subtle*, ערום *arum*, more wise, cunning, or prudent *than any beast of the field which the Lord God had made;* In this account we find: 1. That whatever this *nachash* was, he stood at the head of all inferior animals for wisdom and understanding. 2. That he *walked erect*, for this is necessarily implied in his punishment, — *on thy belly* (*i. e.* on all fours) *shalt thou go*. 3. That he was *endued with the gift of speech;* for a conversation is here related between him and the woman. 4. That he was also endued with the gift of reason, for we find him reasoning and disputing with Eve. 5. That these things were *common* to this creature, the woman no doubt having often seen him walk erect, talk, and reason, and therefore she testifies *no kind of surprise* when he accosts her in the language related in the text; and indeed from the manner in which this is introduced, it appears to be only a part of a conversation that had passed between them on the occasion, — *Yea hath God said*, etc.

"Had this creature never been known to speak before his addressing the woman at this time, and on this subject, it could not have failed to excite her *surprise*, and to have filled her with caution, though from the purity and innocence of her nature, she might have been incapable of being affected with *fear*. Now I apprehend that none of these things can be spoken of a serpent of any species. 1. None of them ever did, or ever *can* walk erect. The tales we have had of two-footed and four-footed serpents, are justly exploded by every judicious naturalist, and are utterly unworthy of credit. The very name of *serpent* comes from *serpo*, to creep; and therefore, to such it could be neither *curse* nor punishment to go on their bellies, *i.e.* to creep on as they had done from their creation; and must do while their race endures. 2. They have no *organs* for *speech*, or any kind of articulate sounds; they can only *hiss*. It is true that an *ass* by miraculous influence, may speak; but it is not to be supposed that there was any miraculous interference here. God did not qualify this creature with speech for the occasion, and it is not intimated that there was any other agent that did it; on the contrary, the text intimates, that *speech* and *reason* were natural to the *nachash;* and is it not in reference to this, the inspired penman says: *The nachash was more subtle or intelligent than all the beasts of the field which the Lord God had made?*

"Nor can I find that the serpentine genus are remarkable for intelligence. It is true, *the wisdom of the serpent* has passed into a proverb, but I can not see on what it is founded, except in reference to the passage in question, where the *nachash* which we translate *serpent,* following the Septuagint, shows so much intelligence and cunning; and it is very probable, that our Lord alludes to this very place when he exhorts his disciples to be *wise,* prudent, or intelligent, as *serpents,* φρονιμοι ὡς οἱ οφεις·; and it is worthy of remark, that he uses the same term employed by the Septuagint, in the text in question, Οφις ἠν φρονιμωτατος, *the serpent was more prudent* or *intelligent* than all the beasts, etc. All these things considered, we are obliged to seek for some other word to designate the *nachash* in the text, than the word *serpent,* which on every view of the subject appears to me inefficient and inapplicable. We have seen above that *khanas, akhanas,* and *khanoos* signify a creature of the *ape* or *satyrus* kind. We have seen that the meaning of the root is, he *lay hid, seduced, slunk away,* etc., and that *khanas* means the *devil,* as the inspirer of evil and the seducer from God and truth. (See

Golius and Wilmet.) It therefore appears to me, that a creature of the *ape* or *orang-outang* kind, is here intended; and that Satan made use of this creature as the most proper instrument for the accomplishment of his murderous purposes against the life and soul of man. Under this creature he *lay hid*, and by this creature he *seduced* our first parents, and *drew off* or *slunk away* from every eye but the eye of God. Such a creature answers to every part of the description in the text; it is evident from the structure of its limbs and their muscles, that it might have been originally designed to walk erect, and that nothing less than a sovereign controlling power, could induce them to put down *hands* in every respect formed like those of man, and walk like those creatures whose claw-armed paws prove them to have been designed to walk on all fours. The subtlety, cunning, endlessly varied pranks and tricks of these creatures, show them, *even now*, to be more subtle and more intelligent than any other creature, man alone excepted. Being *obliged* now to walk on all fours, and gather their food from the ground, they are literally obliged to *eat the dust*, and though exceedingly cunning and careful in a variety of instances, to separate that part which is wholesome and proper for food, from that which is not so, in the article of cleanliness, they are lost to all sense of propriety; and though they have every means in their power, of cleansing the aliments they gather off the ground, and from among the dust, yet they never, in their savage state, make use of any, except a slight rub against their side, or with one of their hands, more to see what the article is than to cleanse it. Add to this, their utter aversion to walk upright; it requires the utmost discipline to bring them to it, and scarcely anything irritates them more than to be obliged to do it. Long observation on some of these animals, enables me to state these facts.

"Should any person who may read this note, object against my conclusions because apparently derived from an Arabic word, which is not exactly similar to the Hebrew, though to those who understand both languages, the similarity will be striking; yet, as I do not insist on the *identity* of the terms, though important consequences have been derived from less likely etymologies, he is welcome to throw the whole of this out of account. He may then take up the Hebrew root only, which signifies to *gaze*, to *view attentively*, *pry into*, *inquire narrowly*, etc., and consider the passage that appears to compare the *nachash* to the *babbler*, (Eccles. xx. 11,) and he will soon find, if he have any acquaintance with creatures of this genus, that for *earnest*, *attentive*, *watching*, *looking*, etc., and for *chattering* or *babbling*, they have no fellows in the animal world. Indeed, the ability and propensity to chatter, is all they have left, according to the above hypothesis, of their original gift of speech, of which they appear to have been deprived at the fall, as a part of their punishment.

"I have spent the longer time on this subject: 1. Because it is exceedingly obscure. 2. Because no interpretation hitherto given of it, has afforded me the smallest satisfaction. 3. Because I think the above mode of accounting for every part of the whole transaction, is consistent and satisfactory; and in my opinion, removes many embarrassments, and solves the chief difficulty. It can be no solid objection to the above mode of solution, that Satan, in different parts of the New Testament, is called the *serpent; the serpent that deceived Eve by his subtilty; the old serpent*, etc., for we have already seen that the New Testament writers have borrowed the word from the Septuagint, and that the Septuagint themselves use it in a *vast variety* and *latitude of meaning;* and surely the *orang-outang* is as likely to be the animal in question as נחש *nachash* and οφις *ophis*, are likely to mean at once a *snake*, a *crocodile*, a *hippopotamus*, *fornication*, a *chain*, a *pair of fetters*, a *piece of brass*, a *piece of steel*, and a *conjurer*; for we have seen above, that all these are acceptations of the original word. Besides, the New Testament writers seem to lose sight of the animal or instrument used on the occasion, and speak only of Satan himself, as the cause of the transgression and the instrument of all evil. If however, any person should choose to differ from the opinion stated above, he is at perfect liberty to do so; I make it no article of faith, nor of Christian communion. I crave the same liberty to judge for myself, that I give to others, to which every man has an indisputable right, and I hope no man will call me a heretic for departing in this respect from the common opinion, which appears to me to be so embarrassed as to be altogether unintelligible."

"[Ver. 14.] The *tempter* is not asked *why he deceived the woman;* he can not roll the blame on any other; *self-tempted he fell*, and it is natural for him, such is his enmity to deceive and destroy all he can. His fault admits of no excuse, and therefore God begins to pronounce the sentence on *him* first. And here we must consider a two-fold sentence, one on *Satan* and the other on the *agent* he employed. The *nachash*, whom I suppose to have been at the head of all the inferior animals, and in a sort of society and intimacy with man, is to be degraded, entirely banished from human society, and deprived of the gift of speech — *Cursed art thou above all cattle and above every beast of the field* — thou shalt be considered the most contemptible of animals; *upon thy belly shalt thou go* — thou shalt no longer walk erect, but mark the ground equally with thy hands and feet; *and dust shalt thou eat*—though formerly possessed of the faculty to distinguish, choose, and cleanse thy food, thou shalt feel henceforth like the most stupid and abject quadruped, *all the days of thy life* —through all the innumerable generations of thy species. God saw meet to manifest his displeasure against the agent employed in this melancholy business; and perhaps this is founded on the part which the intelligent and subtle *nachash* took in the seduction of our first parents. We see that he was capable of it, and have reason to believe that he became a *willing* instrument.

"[Verse 15.] *I will put enmity between thee and the woman.* This has been generally supposed to apply to a certain enmity subsisting between men and serpents, but this is rather a fancy than a reality. It is yet to be discovered that the serpentine race have any peculiar enmity against mankind, nor is there any proof that men hate serpents *more* than they do other noxious animals. Men have much more enmity to the common rat and magpie than they have to all the serpents in the land, because the former destroy the grain, etc., and serpents in general, far from seeking to do men mischief, flee his approach, and generally avoid his dwelling. If, however, we take the word *nachash* to mean any of the *simia* or *ape* species, we find a more consistent meaning, as there is scarcely an animal in the universe so detested by most *women* as these are; and indeed *men* look on them as continual caricatures of themselves. But we are not to look for merely literal meanings here; it is evident that Satan, who, actuated this creature, is alone intended in this part of the prophetic declaration. God, in his endless mercy, has put enmity between men and him; so that, though all mankind love his *service*, yet all invariably hate *himself*. Were it otherwise, who could be saved? A great point gained toward the conversion of the sinner is to convince him that it is *Satan* he has been serving, that it is to *him* he has been giving up his soul, body, goods, etc.; he starts with horror when this conviction fastens on his mind, and shudders at the thought of being in league with the old murderer. But there is a deeper meaning in the text than even this, especially in these words, *it shall bruise thy head*, or rather הוא *hu*, HE; who? the seed of the *woman:* the person is to come by the *woman*, and by her *alone, without the concurrence of man*. Therefore the address is not to Adam and Eve, but to *Eve alone;* and it was in consequence of this purpose of God that Jesus Christ was born of a *virgin;* this, and this alone, is what is implied in the promise of the *seed of the woman* bruising the head of the serpent. Jesus Christ died to put away sin by the sacrifice of himself, and to destroy *him* who had the power of death, that is, the *devil.* Thus he *bruises his head*—destroys his *power* and *lordship* over mankind, turning them from the power of Satan unto God. [Acts xxvi. 18.] And Satan *bruises his heel*—God so ordered it, that the salvation of men could only be brought about by the *death* of Christ; and even the spiritual seed of our blessed Lord have the heel often bruised, as they suffer persecution, temptation, etc., which may be all that is intended by this part of the prophecy."

Aside from the above reference, intimation respecting the chimpanzee, a species of the simia genus, or now considered a distinct species, may reflect additional consideration to this subject.

"The chimpanzee is a native of the west coast of Africa, where it is said to attain a stature equal to that of a man. It is by some supposed to be not so far removed from the negro as to render conversion of the one into the other at all impossible. But if we compare this creature, which is admitted by all zoologists, to make the nearest approach in its structure to the physical conformation of man, with the very lowest and least intelligent of the human race, we shall find the difference so great, as vastly to outweigh the resemblances, and render several intermediate gradations of development necessary, before we can arrive from the most man-like monkey at the lowest and most ape-like of human beings.

"Like other monkeys, the chimpanzee possesses four hands, that is to say, the hinder feet, instead of being fitted as in man for walking on the ground, are converted into hands to assist him in climbing trees, his ordinary place of abode being among the branches. He progresses in fact very awkwardly when in an upright position, as the sole of his foot can not be brought flat to the ground, and he is obliged to walk merely on the outside of it, with his toes drawn up in a very cramped and uncomfortable position. The thumb of these hinder hands, is by no means so perfect as that of the true hands of the anterior members, but even these, when compared with the same organs in man, will be found very inferior in point of perfection. The thumb is much shorter and incapable of being brought into those varied relations with the other fingers which enable the human hand to perform such a vast variety of operations with so much delicacy and precision. In the form of the head, too, the difference is, perhaps, even still more striking. Instead of the large cranium required to contain the brain of a human being, the chimpanzee, like his congeners, has a flat, retreating forehead, with a large ridge over the eyes for the attachment of the strong muscles of the jaws. In the young animal, the forehead is higher, and the ridge just mentioned far less distinct, so that the creature has then a much more intelligent and amiable aspect than at a later period of its existence; and as most, if not all, the specimens which have been brought alive to Europe, have been young, a false impression of their intelligence and docility and also of their external resemblance to the human race has been produced, for it appears that when arrived at maturity they acquire, along with great powers for mischief, every inclination to employ them. . . . .

"Their human-like form does not prevent them from being eaten by the negroes, who regard a well-cooked chimpanzee as exceedingly palatable food, in spite of a tradition which is said to prevail amongst some of them, the chimpanzees were once members of their own *tribe*, but were expelled for the filthiness and depravity of their habits. In captivity, especially when quite young, the animals are exceedingly docile, and imitate many human actions to great perfection, they will take their food with knife, fork, and spoon, and sometimes appear to prefer using these implements, to conveying the food to their mouths with their hands. They drink from a cup or glass, like a human being, and occasionally evince a very human *predilection for intoxicating liquors*."

This reference to the chimpanzee, furnishes a text or two, worthy of consideration: The tradition of the negroes, that *the chimpanzees were once members of their own tribes, but were expelled for the filthiness and depravity of their habits*, may be true; for God has ordained laws to govern humanity. That there are causes which degrade man toward the beast, is true; and it is equally true that there is no limit beyond which, downward, further cause can not take him. Certain conditions are necessary for the constitution of the being man: Those conditions are — such food, such drink, such employment, such society: If those conditions be rejected through successive generations, the being may still be, but it can not be — MAN. But, rather, ——

It can be
Chimpanzee.

The same lie which was told to Eve, is told at this day: An individual, whose depraved appetite craves such food and drink as is not adapted to the wants of man in his high, exalted nature, says to him whose appetite is not so depraved: These things — vile beer, stale, and artificial wine, gin, rum, man-killer — are all good for food, pleasant to the eyes, and to be desired to make one good and wise!

NOTE 5.—*Page* 73.

And is its fruit mature, and juice expressed,
Yet stale and noxious so that we may have, etc.

THE pure, unfermented juice of the grape is an article of refreshment, and oftentimes very necessary; and it is far from my thought to speak against the use of any thing that God, in his infinite wisdom and goodness, has made for the manifold wants of man. Grapes contain a large ratio of nutritive substance: sugar is one of their principal ingredients; but fermentation changes their saccharine matter into alcohol, which still proves to be a deadly poison, notwithstanding all the efforts put forth to make the world believe that it is *good for food*—and *to be desired* to make one *good and wise!* Besides the injurious quality of fermented wines, when we consider the prevalence of the vile compounds which affect the feature of imitation to them — made up of logwood, rhatanay-root, Brazil-wood, brandy-cowe, extract of almond-cake, cherry-laurel-water, gum benzoin, aloes, tartaric acid, lamb's blood, black sloes, sugar of lead! — who will deny that even man — the frail worm — can work miracles by making of deadly poisons, a liquor, which — even while it kills — convinces the appetite that it is *good for food*, and pleasant to the eyes, and *to be desired* to make one *good and wise?*

NOTE 6.—*Page* 78.

Cursed be Canaan, a servant he,
Of servants shall unto his brethren be.

" Instead of *Canaan* simply, the Arabic version has *Ham, the father of Canaan;* but this is acknowledged by none of the other versions." CLARKE.

It seems probable that Ham and his son Canaan, were habitually very intemperate, and that Noah, from the knowledge of the hereditary effects of the same, pronounced the curse on their posterity. " 'The words in the original,' says *Hewlett,* 'are only *cursed Canaan,* equivalent to *wretched, ill-fated Canaan!*' and might not have been spoken till Noah's death." [ED. *Comprehensive Commentary.*]

By the meaning of the text and the context, it is obvious that it was not a single act of Ham nor his son Canaan, in reference to Noah, for which either would incur a curse, himself individually, nor bring on his posterity a curse having no immediate connection with the cause —but their acts must have been such as would necessarily bring a curse on their posterity. Dr. Clarke says that " Ham and, very probably his son Canaan, had treated their father on this occasion with contempt or reprehensible levity." Be that as it was, it is not even supposable that such act, aside from the depravity to cause it, would fix a curse on their multiplied descendants at this day; the meaning is plain: *God shall enlarge Japheth*— *his posterity; and he shall dwell in the tents of Shem;* his posterity shall dwell in the tents of Shem's posterity; *and Canaan shall be his servant*—the descendants of

Canaan shall serve the descendants of Japheth. If it be, as some commentators tell us on the authority of Dr. Bush, that Shem signifies *name* [renown]; Ham, *burnt*, or *black;* Japheth, *persuasion, enlargement;* Canaan, *extreme humiliation*, it must be supposed that these very names had been indicated by the spirit of prophecy: if otherwise, then it must be conceded that in the account of this occurrence, which was probably written by Moses nearly 900 years afterward, the names *Shem, Ham,* and *Japheth,* were also determined subsequently by the fortunes of their descendants.

If doubt be raised as to Ham's or Canaan's depravity, by the violation of physical law, being the cause of the curse upon their posterity from generation to generation, it must apparently be assumed as a part of its foundation, that such is not a cause as likely to reduce to servitude any race of man; which assumption will receive due consideration whenever sincerely presented.

Note 7.—*Page* 89.

We fain would have all feasting here abound,
But never fasting, since thereby, mankind
Become less subject to our influence.

Fasting is not instituted to do violence to the constitution; for if it were, then the heathen who does violence to himself by tearing his flesh with iron hooks in order to appease the supposed anger of his gods, would thereby indulge in a form of worship equally proper. That kind of fasting which does violence to the normal constituency of the physical man, does the same violence to the mental and moral. Fasting is beneficial whenever its effect is to strengthen the being — the mind — the soul — and bring it to the tension that guards against excess and its concomitant influences. Fasting is beneficial to overcome the diseased state which is caused by indulging the appetite in whatever is injurious, or by indulging it to excess. Fasting is beneficial to overcome the vitiated, depraved, — abnormal — state of the appetite itself. Fasting is beneficial to overcome such diseased state and such vitiated, depraved, — abnormal — state of the appetite, whether it be caused by one's own indulgence, or inherited from father, grandfather, or great-grandfather, or progenitor who lived a thousand years before, or even from Adam himself; — and in this, as well as in all acts of kindness and benevolence, our Savior thought it proper to be exemplar ; for by the record of his acts we find that immediately after he was baptized he was led by the spirit into the wilderness, where he fasted forty days and nights, at which time the devil made unsuccessful attempts to influence him. The moral power of fasting — this great law of nature, of God — Christ taught to his disciples; for when, on a certain occasion they had failed to cast out a devil, and asked him why they could not, he replied that "this kind goeth not out but by prayer and *fasting*."

Piety is promoted by fasting, but sinful desires are augmented by repletion; for whatever clogs the physical functions, affects injuriously the mind and soul, which, with the physical, have mutual relation — therefore, such physical injury is also mental and moral injury: Thereby one becomes less satisfied with himself and those around him, and is in a less fit condition to fulfil the last command of our Savior, *that ye love one another.*

NOTE 8.—*Page* 94.

O, that was Babel—

"THE Targums, both of *Jonathan ben Uzziel* and of *Jerusalem*, assert that the tower was for idolatrous purposes, and that they intended to place an image on the top of the tower, with a sword in its hand probably to act as a talisman against their enemies. Whatever *their* design might have been, it is certain that this temple or tower was afterward devoted to idolatrous purposes. Nebuchadnezzar repaired and beautified this tower, and it was dedicated to *Bel*, or the sun." [CLARKE.]

According to Herodotus, the tower in the temple of Belus in Babylon (supposed to be identical with the tower of Babel) was pyramidal, and each side at the base measured a furlong, making the whole a half mile in circumference; its height, according to the estimation of another, was six hundred and sixty feet. Forty years after Babylon had been conquered by Cyrus, Xerxes, after having plundered the city, laid this temple in ruins: It is the most stupendous mass of all that remains of Babylon. It lies in a desert about six miles from Hilleh; The ruins of this temple are called *Birs Nimrood*: The Jews call it Nebuchadnezzar's prison. With respect to the identity of the tower of Babel, however, there are different opinions.

NOTE 9.—*Page* 94.

For Nimrod hunted men — made them depart
From the teachings far of Shem's posterity.

DR. Adam Clarke, referring to Nimrod (Gen. x. 8), says: "Of this person little is known, as he is not mentioned except here and in 1 Chron. i. 10, which is evidently a copy of the text in Genesis. He is called *a mighty hunter before the Lord;* and from verse 10, we learn that he founded a *kingdom* which included the cities *Babel, Erech, Accad, and Calneh, in the land of Shinar.* Though the words are not definite, it is very likely he was a very bad man. His name (Nimrod) comes from מרד *marad, he rebelled*; and the Targum on 1 Chron. i. 10, says: *Nimrod began to be a mighty man in sin, a murderer of innocent men and a rebel before the Lord.* The Jerusalem Targum says: 'He was mighty in hunting [or in prey] and in sin before God; for he was a hunter of the children of men in their languages; and he said unto them, *Depart from the religion of Shem and cleave to the institutes of Nimrod.*' The Targum of Jonathan ben Uzziel says: 'From all the foundation of the world, none was ever found like Nimrod, powerful in hunting, and in rebellions against the Lord.' The Syriac calls him *a warlike giant.* The ציד *tsayid,* which we render *hunter,* signifies *prey;* and is applied in the Scriptures to the hunting of men by persecution, oppression, and tyranny. Hence it is likely that Nimrod, having acquired power, used it in tyranny and oppression; and by rapine and violence, founded that domination which was the first distinguished by the name of a *kingdom* on the face of the earth. How many kingdoms have been founded in the same way, in various ages and nations from that time to the present! From the Nimrods of the earth, God deliver the world!"

NOTE 10. — *Page* 101.

Do this one thing — fall down and worship me.

"THE last temptation was the most subtle and the most powerful — *All these will I give thee if thou wilt fall down and worship me. To inherit all nations,* had been repeatedly declared to be the birth-right of the Messiah. His right to *universal empire* could not be controverted; nor could Satan presume to make the investiture. What then, was his purpose? Satan had hitherto opposed, and that with considerable success, the Kingdom of God on the earth; and what he appears to propose here, were *terms of peace* and an *honorable retreat.* The *worship* which he exacted was an act of *homage* in return for his cession of that *ascendency* which, through the sin of man, he had obtained in the world. Having long established his rule among men, it was not at first to be expected, that he would resign it without a combat; but the purpose of this last temptation appears to be an offer to decline any further contest; and yet more, if his terms were accepted, apparently to engage his influence to promote the kingdoms of the Messiah. And as the condition of this proposed alliance, he required, *not divine worship,* but such an *act of homage* as implied *amity* and *obligation;* and if this construction be allowed, he may be supposed to have enforced the necessity of the measure, by every suggestion of the *consequences of a refusal.* The sufferings which would inevitably result from a provoked opposition which would render the victory, though certain to Christ himself, dearly bought; added to which, the conflict he was prepared to carry on through succeeding ages, in which all his subtlety and powers should be employed to hinder the progress of Christ's cause in the earth, and that with a considerable degree of anticipated success. There the devil seems to propose to make over to Christ the power and influence he possessed in this world on *condition* that he would enter into terms of peace with him; and the inducement offered was, that thereby our Lord should *escape those sufferings* both in his *own person,* and in those of his adherents, which a provoked contest would insure. And we may suppose that a similar temptation lies hid in the desires excited even in some of the servants of Christ, who may feel themselves often induced to employ *worldly* influences and power for the promotion of his kingdom, even though, in so doing, an apparent commission of Christ and Belial is the result: for it will be found, that neither wordly riches, nor power, can be employed in the service of Christ, till, like the spoils taken in war, (Deut. xxxi. 21–23,) they have passed through the fire and water, as, without a divine purification, they are not fit to be employed in the service of God and his Church.

"Hence we may conclude that the first temptation had for its professed object: 1. Our Lord's *personal relief* and *comfort,* through the inducement of a *separate* and *independent* act of power. The second temptation professed to have in view his *public acknowledgment by the people* as the MESSIAH; for should they see him work such a miracle as throwing himself down from the pinnacle of the temple without receiving any hurt, they would be led instantly to acknowledge his divine mission; and the *evil* of this temptation may be explained, as seeking to secure the success of his mission by other means than those, which, as the Messiah, he had received from the Father. Compare John xiv. 31. The *third* temptation was a subtle attempt to induce Christ to acknowledge Satan as an *ally* in the establishment of his kingdom."—E. M. B.

"The above is the substance of the ingenious theory of my correspondent, which may be considered as a *third* mode of interpretation partaking equally of the *allegoric* and *literal.*" — CLARKE.

NOTE 11.—*Page* 103.

A soldier offers him vinegar in a sponge on a reed.

THIS *vinegar* was doubtless the *wine mingled with myrrh* which they had offered him a short time previously. (John xix. 29.) "Now there was set a vessel," etc.—the one containing the mixture offered him on this *previous occasion*—Mark xv. 23. "And they gave him wine mingled with myrrh; but he received it not." The parallel place in Matthew (xxvii. 34) has: "They gave him vinegar to drink mingled with gall; and when he had tasted thereof, he would not drink." In allusion to the second time it was offered him, John has (xix. 30): "When JESUS therefore had *received* the vinegar, he said: 'It is finished:" — It is very probable that he only *tasted*, and then *refused* it as he had previously done; for in the parallel passages we find that others objected, and perhaps somewhat restrained the one who offered him the vinegar probably to revive him, that they might see if *Elias* would come and save him from the power of his enemies (Matthew, xxvii. 48–49): "And straightway one of them ran and took a sponge, and filled it with vinegar, and put it on a reed and gave him to drink. The *rest* said, Let be, let us see whether Elias will come and save him." (Mark xv. 36): "And one ran and filled a sponge full of vinegar, and put it on a reed and gave him to drink, saying, Let alone; let us see whether Elias will come to take him down." There is probably an omission in the text here; for, according to the other evangelists who have spoken of this, it was not he who offered him the vinegar, but the *rest* who said, *Let alone*, etc. Luke speaks of the vinegar only as having been *offered* to him (chap. xxiii. 36, 37): "And the soldiers also mocked him, coming to him and offering him vinegar, and saying, If thou be the King of the Jews, save thyself."

Clarke tells us that "Inebriating drinks were given to condemned prisoners, to render them less sensible of the torture they endured in dying. — This custom of giving stupifying potions to condemned malefactors, is alluded to in Proverbs xxxi. 6. *Give strong drink.* שכר *shekar,* inebriating drink, *to him who is ready to perish.* i.e. to him who is condemned to death; *and wine to him who is* BITTER *of soul* — because he is just going to suffer the punishment of death, and thus the Rabbins understand it." (*Clarke's Commentary Note,* Matt. xxvii. 34. Prov. v. 34.)

"The Talmud, states that this drink consisted of wine mixed with frankincense, and was given to criminals immediately before execution. A preparation of this kind was offered to our Savior: 'And they gave him to drink, wine mingled with myrrh, but he received it not.' The same custom was observed among the Romans, and, at a comparatively recent period, a similar practice prevailed in some part of this country [England]."—GRINROD.

NOTE 12.—*Page* 113.

For from the fruits of th' earth is death distilled.

THERE are different opinions respecting the time when distillation was first discovered. Professor Waterhouse says: "The art of procuring ardent spirit by distillation was the discovery of the Arabian chemists, a century or two after the death of Mahomet, who died in 631. But so sensible were the Mahometans of the destructive effects of spirituous liquors that the use of them was prohibited even by their own laws. Such, however, was their prejudice against Christianity, that they willingly suffered this infernal and fascinating spirit to be introduced among Christian nations. *A more subtle plan, perhaps, could not have been devised to eradicate every religious principle from the human mind, and to disseminate those of an opposite nature.* A considerable time had elapsed before ardent spirits were manufactured in Europe, and they were very sparingly used for several centuries. Then, people in general were exempted from raging disorders both of body and mind. In process of time, however, when distilled spirits were freely taken, it was observed that new diseases appeared, and such disorders as had been mild and tractable became formidable and alarming."

Grinrod tells us (*Bacchus, a Prize Essay*) that "the date and authors of this invention [distillation,] are involved in considerable obscurity. The Chinese, whose perseverance in scientific pursuits are well known, are, by some writers, supposed to have been acquainted at an early period with the art of distillation. This supposition, however, is destitute of the necessary proofs.

"The Chinese and Saracens had long been acquainted with a species of distillation, by means of which they were enabled to extract the essence or *aroma* of flowers. Perfumes and essences were held in great esteem by these oriental nations.

"Pliny, who flourished in the first century of the Christian era, does not make the slightest allusion to the art of distillation. Galen is also silent on this subject. This justly celebrated physician flourished about a century after Pliny. Galen alludes to distillation as a means of extracting the aroma of plants and flowers.

"The same observation will apply to the Arabians, who were famed for their pretended knowledge of alchemy and the profession of medicine. Rhazes, Albucassis, and Avicenna, three celebrated physicians who lived about the tenth and eleventh centuries, speak of the distillation of roses, but not of the extraction of intoxicating spirit from fermented liquors.

"Arnoldus de Villa or Villanova, a physician of the south of Europe, who flourished in the thirteenth century, is the first writer who distinctly alludes to the discovery of ardent spirit. From the statements of this member of the medical profession, it appears that the ancients were not acquainted with the process—that it had only become recently known."

NOTE 13.—*Page* 114.

This is the universal panacea,
The emanation of divinity.

ARNOLDUS DE VILLA informs us that when ardent spirit was discovered, it was supposed to be a "universal *panacea.*" Raymond Lully of Majorca, who was a disciple of Arnoldus de Villa, dwelt with much animation on its supposed medicinal properties; indeed, he supposed it to be "an emanation of divinity sent for the physical renovation of mankind. It is said that he first applied to it the name of *alcohol.*

In Hollinshed's Chronicles, there is an allusion to a treatise by Theoricus, which speaks thus of the medicinal properties of alcohol: "It sloweth age, it strengtheneth youth, it helpeth digestion, it cutteth phlegme, it abandoneth melancholic, it relisheth the heart, it lighteneth the mind, it quickeneth the spirits, it cureth the hydropsia, it healeth the strangurie——it puffeth away ventositie, it keepeth and preserveth the head from whirring, the eyes from dazzling, the tongue from lisping, the mouth from snaffling, the teeth from chattering, and the throat from rattling; it keepeth the weasan from stiffling, the stomach from wambling, and the heart from swelling;—it keepeth the hands from shivering, the sinews from shrinking, the veins from crumbling, the bones from aching, and the marrow from soaking."

NOTE 14.—*Page* 119.

And the Christians shall carry it to the heathen nations.

I KNOW not what reflects so severely upon Christian nations as the extension of the means and habitude of intemperance to the heathen at the same time and often in deplorable connection with what they offer as the Christian religion. The efforts of the missionary have often been paralysed to a very great extent by the influences promoting intemperance, which have often accompanied their labors among the heathen, who, if left without the aid of those efforts associated with such evil, would be, indeed, less the objects of commiseration.

Grinrod tells us, on authorities to which he refers, that "it was no uncommon thing in Calcutta, and other places, to see a European lie intoxicated in the street, surrounded by several natives who were very scrupulous in the observance of their religious rites and ceremonies, and to hear them tauntingly exclaim: 'Here is one of your Europeans, look at him, you never see us get drunken, as you do; let your missionaries stop at home and preach to their own countrymen?' . . . .

"The simple Indian can not forbear to reproach his religious instructor with an inconsistency so glaringly opposed to the principles of humanity; and much more of Christianity. 'I am glad,' said a missionary to an Indian chief, 'that you do not drink whisky, but it grieves me to find that your people are accustomed to use so much of it.' 'Ah, yes,' said the red man, as he fixed an eloquent eye upon the preacher, which communicated the reproof before he uttered it—'We Indians *use* a great deal of whisky: but we do not make it!'

"Scarcely any tribe among the untutored Indians in North America, has been free from the consequences arising from the introduction and use of alcoholic liquors. The records of missionary labors among those tribes exhibit in the strongest light the obstacles which this demoralizing practice presents to the introduction and diffusion of religious truth.

"The same injurious example is found to exist among professing Christians in Mahometan countries, and is productive of corresponding impressions on the followers of the prophet. The remarks of a respected missionary in Persia, are to the point: 'What kind of Christianity do the Mahometans of this country behold? *None that has life*—none that is productive of a *morality*, even *equal* to their own;' intemperance, for instance, is so common among the *Christians* of Persia, and the few Europeans who stroll hither for the sake of lucre, that where Mahometans see one of their own sect intoxicated, which is now become rather common, they at once say, 'That man has left Mahomet and gone over to Jesus.'

"The same observation may be applied to China. The Chinese view with great jealousy the introduction of foreign customs, and in particular the attempts made to convert them to Christianity. These strong prejudices have no doubt, been greatly strengthened by the intemperate conduct of the inhabitants of Christian countries, occasionally residing among them. In the year 1831, the Chinese authorities at Canton, had occasion to issue a proclamation forbidding the sale of wine and spirits to foreign seamen. This measure originated in the intemperate conduct of European and American seamen, who, in their fits of intoxication frequently disturbed the public peace, and this to so serious an extent, as to cause a suspension of commercial intercourse between China and European nations. Lamentable indeed must be that state of things, by which the government of a heathen territory is compelled to restrain the immorality of natives of a Christian land.

"The inconsistent conduct of professing Christians exhibits a similar result in regard to the exertions now being made for the conversion of the posterity of Abraham. It can, therefore, excite little surprise that these efforts have, hitherto, in a great measure been ineffectual. These remarks more particularly apply to Poland and Russia. The affecting appeal of a recently converted Jew to his Christian friends, can not be too extensively read. He distinctly shows that the inconsistency of Christian professors forms the main obstacle to the conversion of the Jews. 'In the better classes of society on the continent, there is, as I have already said, more strictness of morals among the Jews, than among the Christians.' 'The immorality of the Christian is quite proverbial among the Jews.' Again: 'You may imagine what I felt, when, inquiring one day of my brother, concerning an old acquaintance, he replied, without having any intention to offend me, or even reflecting how his answer was likely to affect me, "He lives exactly like a Christian;" meaning that he led a profligate life.' Also, still in relation to the conduct of Christians abroad: 'The Jews are aware that Christians have as well as they, a day which is called their Sabbath, and various other festivals or holy days. How do they behold these days professedly devoted to the service of Christ, spent by his pretended worshippers. They see the country part of the population coming in to join their brethren of the towns in the services of the church, and after these are over, they see them resort to the public houses, not merely to spend the rest of the day in rioting and drunkenness, but even in the commission of crimes, etc.' The narrative is too revolting to be further detailed."

It was quite recently that England made war on China because the Chinese had refused to be stultified—killed, by their opium. To-day we have news of the bombardment of Canton by British war-vessels, the opportunity for which appears to have been sought in the pretense of *insulted flag;* yet while the real cause plainly appears to be the exclusiveness of the Governor General Yeh, "who," the *London Leader* informs us, "appears to belong to the high tory party of the celestial empire—that party which would for ever shut the 'central flower nation' against barbaric intruders like the vulgar British." For at least a moiety of this exclusiveness, is not the British nation responsible? Let the ghosts of the Celestials who have been killed by British opium, give answer!

It appears that the American nation has not been behind in affording to the heathen the means of intoxication. "During the year 1835, fourteen merchant-vessels eleven of which were American, sold in the port of Honolulu, Island of Mani, alone, 16,950 gallons of ardent spirits, and carried 37,522 gallons to the Indians of the northwest coast, making 54,000 gallons of rum and brandy distributed among the natives, and it was ascertained that the largest proportion of this was shipped by a *deacon* of a congregational church in Boston. New England rum has found its way from California to Behring's Straits, among all the islands of the Pacific and Indian oceans, and it has even penetrated into Africa, Egypt, and through the whole extent of the Sultan's dominions.—The rum which has been exported from this country has usually been diluted with one-half water, then drugged with tobacco, pepper, etc., and sold for about four dollars per gallon.—Not long since, the barque Emma Isadora, sailed from Boston with a cargo of 5,200 gallons of rum and several missionaries for the heathen!"—LEE.

This is lamentable to consider; yet it will ever be thus while professed Christians neglect to enforce the true teachings of Christ by the powerful presentation, (both by precept and example) of God's law, which is recognized in nature, and which man must recognize, or pay the terrible penalty of disobedience and infidelity.

NOTE 15.—*Page* 119.

I know not why, unless it be from suspicion that on the western world will arise influences more powerful than any yet, to oppose the good-vile liquors.

GOVERNMENTS and religious orders have, at different times, enacted laws to restrain intemperance, the most remarkable and effective of which, I will here, on the authority of Grinrod, present mention:

"The religion of the Chinese, and of most neighboring nations, enjoins upon its devoted followers entire abstinence from all intoxicating liquors. The inhabitants of China generally, as well as the natives of Japan, adopt the religious creed of the divinity *Fo*, whose precepts, by a strict conformity to which alone, they conceive they can lead a virtuous life, and obtain his approbation, are as follows: 1st. Not to kill anything that has life. 2dly. Not to steal. 3dly. Not to commit fornication. 4thly. Not to lie. And 5thly. *Not to drink strong liquors.*"

"The doctrines of Boodh, or Budha, are adopted by nearly one half of the human race. In Ceylon, the Birman empire, Siam and Laos, this imaginary deity is worshipped under the name of *Godama* or *Gautama;* throughout China under the name of *Fo*, and in Japan, by the name of *Siaka*. The following quotation illustrates the command of this Chinese divinity: — This law commands us not to drink any intoxicating liquor. There are many sorts in the western frontier countries, as liquors made of sugar-cane, of grapes, and of many other plants; in this country (China) it is the general custom to make a strong liquor from rice — of all these thou shalt not drink, with this exception, when thou art sick, and nothing else can restore thy health, and then it must be known by all that thou drink strong liquors. If there be reason for it thou shalt not touch any liquor with thy lips, thou shalt not bring it to thy nose to smell at, nor shalt thou sit in a tavern, or together with people who drink spirits.

"There was once a certain Yew-pohan, who, by breaking this law, violated also all others, and committed the thirty-six sins; you can see by this, that it is no small sin to drink wine [strong drink.] There is a particular department in hell filled with mire and dirt for the transgressors of this law, and they will be born again as stupid and mad people, wanting wisdom and intelligence. There are bewildering demons and maddening herbs, but spirits disorder the mind more than any poison. The Scripture moveth us, therefore, to drink melted copper, sooner than violate this law and drink spirits. Ah, how watchful ought we to be ourselves." — *Catechism of the Shamas, or the Laws and Regulations of the Priesthood of Budha.*

The very remarkable and successful attempt in the Mahometan faith, to arrest the evil of intemperance is said to have originated not with the prophet Mahomet, but to have been taken from a sacred book called the *Taalim*, the author of which gives the following reason for the enactment of prohibition from the use of wine:

"Two angels, the one called Arot, and the other Marot, were sent in preference to all others to govern the world, with express orders not to drink wine. A difference happening to arise between a husband and wife, who previously had lived together in the greatest harmony; the latter who was desirous to regain the affections of her husband, imagined that she could easily accomplish so desirable an object by the mediation of the two favorites of Heaven. She accordingly invited them to her house, where they were received with every mark of distinction. Wine was presented to them in a cup, which they were not able to refuse from the beautiful hands that offered it. 'It is not,' remarks the writer, from whose work this narration is taken, 'very excusable in celestial beings to become mortal for the sake of a fine woman.' They tasted of the liquor which seemed so delicious in its nature, that they drank too much of it, so that becoming inflamed, and even intoxicated by it, they were desirous to repay their kind hostess by certain marks of attachment, which, remarks the same writer, are in general more used by lovers than by husbands. The woman being faithful and chaste, was much embarrassed and concerned to get out of this dilemma. Under a pretense of curiosity, however, she asked the two messengers what words they made use of to procure a return to heaven. One weakness generally leads to another, and the angels disclosed to her their important secret. The woman instantly profited by their disclosure, and ascended to the throne of the Eternal, where, in a suppliant tone, she exposed her complaint which was heard with justice. The Father of the Universe did even more, for this pure soul became a radiant star, and the faithful angels were tied by the feet with chains, and precipitated into the well called Babil, where the Mahometans believe they will remain until the day of judgment. The Almighty, on this account, prohibited the use of wine to all his servants for ever.

"The less learned among the Mahometans, attribute this celebrated law to the following circumstance: — One day, Mahomet, passing through a village, remarked that the inhabitants were celebrating some festival with great joy. Having ascertained that a wedding and wine were the cause of this mirth, the prophet in his wisdom, judging that pleasure was the soul of life, conceived a great fondness for that liquor, which enchanted the senses, by making men forget their miseries. On passing, however, the next morning through the same place, Mahomet saw the earth drenched with human blood, and soon learned that the guests having become mad by their excessive use of wine, had attacked each other in the most cruel manner, and some of them had been killed, while the greater part were covered with wounds. The prophet, like a wise man, now saw reason to change his former hasty opinion, and determined to have nothing to do with a custom, the end of which was so bitter and destructive."

"In the 17th century, it would appear that the Turks had acquired a love for wine, for, according to Sir Paul Ricaut, the Sultan Amurath, A.D. 1634, forbade entirely the use of wine, and punished several with death for disobeying his order. A similar edict was issued by Mahomet the Fourth, A.D. 1670, who commanded all those who had any wine to send it out of the town, and the punishment of death was announced as the penalty of disobedience. The edict of this emperor was generally carried into execution. In the decree in question, Mahomet spoke of wine as a most noxious liquor, invented by the devil to destroy the souls of men, to disturb their reason, and to inflame their passions. This monarch was, no doubt, influenced in his conduct by the terrible seditions occasioned by wine in the reign of Mahomet the Third. The latter had his seraglio forced by his soldiers, who were under the influence of wine, and escaped with his own life by the sacrifice of his principal favorite.

"Similar prohibitions have frequently been enforced in more modern times in Mahometan countries. In Sudan, for instance, the Sultan Abdelrahman, in 1795, prohibited the use of intoxicating liquor, under the penalty of death, and those who made it, had their heads shaved, and were publicly exposed to every possible degradation. In Persia also, during Sir Robert Ker Porter' visit to that country, in 1819 and 1820, a severe prohibition was made against wine by the reigning monarch, who not only himself abstained from its use, but ordered his officers to destroy all the wine they could discover in any part of the kingdom.

"The late Sultan died of *delirium tremens*, the result of vinous indulgence. The present Sultan, his son, on his accession to the throne, issued a proclamation against the use of wine, and caused one million of piasters worth of wine to be thrown into the Bosphorus."

NOTE 16.—*Page* 132.

Ay, this is th' very secret of our rule:
With vile destructive essences do we
Contaminate the very blood of life,
And thus develop in the being man,
The most unnatural predominance
Of faculties, which, yielding to our sway,
Urge the pursuit of evil, and in shade
So deep shroud him that he will not, nor dare
Seek light!

I regard this as being emphatically affirmed in the Holy Bible, and all nature, of which God is the author: it is concomitant of every law that he has uttered for the government of man, or else it is not true that matter can affect the soul for good or evil; and if that is not true, then it is not true that "No drunkard can inherit the kingdom of heaven." By the influence of *matter* the soul may receive harm though the indulgence be not that which determines *drunkenness.* The laws of God are in the constitution of man, and he who is ignorant of man, is ignorant of theology.

The laws of man's being are spiritual, social and physical.

When man is in his moral state as a spiritual being, his spirit is in communion with God.

When man is in his normal state as a social being, his acts are such as contribute to the happiness of himself and those around him.

When man is in his normal state as a physical being, he lives in obedience to the physical law as *required by the normal spirit.*

To be in the normal state physically, is to be prepared for obedience to the social and spiritual laws of the being.

To be in the normal state socially, is the result of being in the normal state physically and spiritually.

To be in the normal state spiritually, is to be in spiritual communion with God, the proof of which will be such love to man as is manifest in fulfilling the social law, and neither of these can be, while the being is not in the normal state physically — for the holy spirit of God can not dwell in an unfit temple.

All the laws of man's being are so instituted that the violation of them brings its own punishment.

Man having been created with his spirit in communion with the spirit of God, he is ever unhappy while his spirit is not in such communion.

Man having been created a social being, he is ever unhappy while he does not conform to all that is required of him as such.

Man having been created a physical being, he is ever unhappy while he does not fulfill the laws that govern him as such:——therefore,

A man can not be happy spiritually without his spirit being in communion with God, any more than he can be happy physically while his hand is in the fire.

All punishment is designed for good: the pain that is felt when the hand is in the fire, is to cause the hand to be taken out quickly. The pain that the spirit feels when banished from God, is to bring him back to God, or else its purpose must be only for example.

God never gave evil propensities to man; he came by them, from the violation of law by himself or his progenitors — the same way that he comes by dyspepsia and gout.

" What from this barren being do we reap,
Our senses narrow and our reason frail,
Life short, and truth a gem that loves the deep,
And all things weighed in custom's falsest scale:
Opinion is omnipotence, whose veil
Mantles the earth with darkness until right
And wrong are *accidents*, and men grow pale
Lest their own judgments should become too bright,
And their free thoughts be crimes, and earth have too much light."

NOTE 17.—*Page* 133.

In the establishment in Africa
Of such Christianity as doth receive
And cherish in its range the evil fruit.

ACCORDING to the account given by Mungo Park, who travelled in Africa in the years 1795, 1796, and 1797, the Africans who are converted to the Mahometan faith, drink nothing but water; and considering the intemperance generally existing in Christian nations, it is quite probable that the enemy of mankind prefers that the Africans be converted to the religion that admits the use of intoxicating liquors as a beverage, rather than that they become Mahometans.

NOTE 18.—*Page* 134.

Strifes, wars, havoc, and the imbibing of intoxicating mead.

"THE honey which they collect is chiefly used by themselves in making a strong, *intoxicating liquor*, much the same as the mead which is produced from the honey in Great Britain."

"If a man loses his life in one of those sudden quarrels which perpetually occur at their feasts, when the whole party is *intoxicated with mead*, his sons," etc.

"The beverage of the Pagan Negroes is *beer* and *mead;* of each of which they frequently drink to excess." —*Mungo Park's Travels in Africa.*

NOTE 19.—*Page* 135.

I will bring hither votaries of Baccho
And Mammon, in effective complement.

THE reader can see how effectually this determination has been carried out. The greater share of the low groggeries that curse this land, are kept by individuals who have migrated here, not to bless our country, but to enlarge upon it the curse of intemperance. It is not agreeable to make this charge, but it is true, especially as regards the cities. We welcome you, foreigners—to engage in any occupation that is for the good of our country, but if you love the country of your adoption, seek, rather, to assist us to relieve it of the greatest evil that can afflict any land.

NOTE 20.—*Page* 135.

Fast into port at Jamestown, and a score
Of Africans I there have set on shore
And sold them.

IN the year 1620, a Dutch vessel arrived at Jamestown in Virginia, having aboard twenty Negroes who were there sold for slaves. This was the beginning of slavery within what was then the boundary of the British Colonies in America.

NOTE 21.—*Page* 137.

And yet the strife of arms has much enhanced
Intoxication by the essences
From the West Indies.

THE time of this scene is shortly after the close of the French war. The Hon. Charles A. Lee, in alluding to the intemperance at this time and during many years previous, says: "Between the years 1700 and 1750, West India rum began to come into very general use, especially in New England and New York, among the farmers and laboring men. The lumber and produce of the entire colonies were bartered for the products of the West Indies; and it was not unusual at this period, for farmers to consume from one to two barrels of rum in a year.

The French war also which occurred about this period had a most disastrous effect on the habits of the people, in respect to the use of spirituous liquors. This war commenced in 1755 and terminated in 1763, having lasted eight years. The colonies furnished the principal portion of the troops although considerable bodies were sent over from England, many of whom had served in the low countries, where spirit was in general use. Rations were accordingly served out and thus thousands of New England men who had never been addicted to its use, acquired a taste and a habit of drinking which followed them on their return to their own families."

NOTE 22.—*Page* 140.

The curmi or the mil-fion.

CURMI (ale) we are told was the peculiar drink of the ancient Irish and Britons. Mil-fion (mead) is said to have been the common beverage of the early inhabitants of England.

NOTE 23.—*Page* 140.

The people of Albion be also a nation of drunkards.

IT appears that the English had become particularly noted for drunkenness; indeed, during the period that England was a commonwealth, drunkenness was so common that it was called by other nations the Land of Drunkards. In the Historical Miscellany, Gentlemen's Magazine, 1736, there is notice of grog-shops having the inviting sign: "Drunk for a penny, dead drunk for two pence, clean straw for nothing." Smollet in the History of England, in alluding to this fact says: "They accordingly provided cellars and places strewed with straw, to which they conveyed those wretches who were overwhelmed with intoxication. In those dismal caverns they lay until they recovered some use of their faculties, and then they had recourse to the same mischievous potion; thus consuming their health and ruining their families, in hideous receptacles of the most filthy vice, resounding with riot, execration, and blasphemy."

Shakspeare, in alluding to the noted drunkenness of the English, places in the mouth of Hamlet in tragedy, the following acknowledgment:

> "This heavy-headed revel east and west
> Makes us traduced and taxed of other nations;
> They clepe us, drunkards, and with swinish phrase
> Soil our addition; and, indeed, it takes
> From our achievements, though performed at hight,
> The pith and marrow of their attribute."

We learn on good authority (see Bartholin, lib. ii. c. 12) that intemperance abounded even in their religious festivals (?), on which occasions they drank largely to the honor of the Apostles, of the Virgin Mary, and of Christ!

NOTE 24.—*Page* 154.

There is a cave, and near its opening, etc.

SOME may suppose that the Mammoth Cave in Kentucky is here meant; yet I must acknowledge that I am not aware that tradition or history gives any account of the infernals having occupied this place for their deliberations; however, in this great and wonderful cavern there are some scenes which are known by very significant names: I may mention *The Bottomless Pit, The Haunted Chamber, Purgatory, The River Styx.* At the distance of nearly six miles in the cave, is a *sulphur spring*, and near it, a huge pile of empty *wine-bottles.*

NOTE 25.—*Page* 179.

A country in Pennsylvania.—Enter a body of Insurgents, etc.

"SOON after the adoption of the Federal Constitution, Congress enacted a general excise law, which was peculiarly obnoxious to those who had opposed the adoption of the Constitution. Such was especially the case with the inhabitants west of the Alleghany Mountains, who openly denounced the excise law as tyrannical, unnecessary, and unjust, and those who voted for it, as the friends of monarchy and the enemies of a republican government. Being far removed from any market, they found it more profitable to distil than to export the products of the soil, and in September, 1791, open combinations began to be formed for resisting the enforcement of the law. Many of the collectors were tarred and feathered, and other indignities offered them, so that no persons could be found who were willing to undertake the office. The deputy marshals were also intimidated from serving process on those who had committed acts of violence on the persons of revenue officers. The most obnoxious features of the excise act were repealed by Congress; but still it could not be enforced. The *principle* of excise, and not the detail of its execution, became the object of hostility. A general convention was held at Pittsburgh, at which resolutions, for the second time were passed, for resisting the execution of the law, for withholding all intercourse with excise officers, and for treating them on all occasions with contempt. The people at large were exhorted to follow the same line of conduct; committees of correspondence were appointed, and pains taken to increase the number of the disaffected.

"At first the President issused a proclamation, exhorting all persons to desist from any combination or proceedings which tended to obstruct the execution of the laws, and require the interference of the civil magistrates. Other measures were also adopted, such as intercepting spirits on their way to market, and directing the agents of the army to purchase only those on which the duty had been paid. But notwithstanding all these measures, the law was still resisted until the 15th of July, 1794, the marshal, while in the execution of his duty, was beset on the road by a body of armed men, who fired at him. On the next day, the insurgents, to the number of five hundred, attacked the house of the inspector, and took him prisoner, together with the force which he had collected for his defense. The public mails from Pittsburgh to Philadelphia, were stopped and rifled, and the insurgents boldly proclaimed that it was their intention to resist by force of arms the authority of the United States. No other alternative being now left, the President of the United States made a requisition on the Governors of New Jersey, Pennsylvania, Maryland, and Virginia, for a force of 15,000 men, who were placed under the command of Governor Lee, of Virginia. The insurgents numbered about 7,000 strong. The army marched into the country of the disaffected, but finding no armed force but what was readily dispersed, left a small body of men after having secured a few of the leaders, and thus ended the famous WHISKY REBELLION of 1791." —LEE.

NOTE 26.—*Page* 185.

——A gleam
Of light shot out of heaven athwart the ways
Of our dominion.

THIS is allusion to the temperance movement in the United States. The "American Temperance Society" was instituted in the year 1826. The labors and writings of the Rev. Dr. Lyman Beecher, doubtless contributed very largely to give impulse to the temperance cause which has moved onward, gathering strength, and saved the country from the ruin which was impending in the vice of intemperance. And if the zeal of philanthropists now be turned away from this evil, our country may yet sink into ruin. Are not the enemies to peace and prosperity, now calling for more of the man-destroying liquor, and for liberty to dispense it; and is not that liberty granted—so that our neighbors, our friends, our sons, our daughters, our grand-children, may suffer from its influence—may starve, and shiver in rags—may DRINK it and be DESTROYED!

NOTE 27.—*Page* 188.

He shall be plied with vilest essences, etc.

I HAVE not deemed it essential that I should adopt the same circumstance of Legree's earlier days, as presented in "Uncle Tom's Cabin," which influenced him to brutalities.—I have not thought it necessary to send him forth upon the ocean in a piratical vessel in order to prepare him for crimes of the grossest nature; no: For this, I find the entire means on dry land:—all the instruments and appliances are there, and it has seemed to me only necessary to present him as being made a subject of their influence. I have done so. That intemperance was the principal cause of the cruelties of Legree, will doubtless appear when we consider the following quotations from "Uncle Tom's Cabin."

"Simon rode on, however, apparently well pleased, occasionally pulling away at a flask in his pocket."—Chap. 32.

"Legree was just mixing himself a tumbler of punch, pouring his hot water from a cracked and broken-nosed pitcher, grumbling as he did so, 'Plague on that Sambo,'" etc.—Chap. 35.

"'Blast it,' said Legree to himself, as he sipped his liquor; 'where did he get that?'"—Ib.

"Legree and both the drivers, in a state of furious intoxication, were singing, whooping, upsetting chairs, and making all manner of ludicrous and horrid grimaces at each other."—Ib.

"His coarse, strong nature craved, and could endure, a continual stimulation, that would have utterly wrecked and crazed a finer one."—Chap. 36.

"Legree was serving brandy profusely among them."—Chap. 40.

"He drank more than usual; held up his head briskly, and swore louder than ever."—Chap. 42.

"After this Legree became a harder drinker than ever before."—Ib.

NOTE 28.—*Page* 225.

—*Think of it and smile.*

MR. DUNLOP, in a work entitled, "Drinking usages in Great Britain," details them to the number of two hundred and ninety-seven!

NOTE 29.—*Page* 253.

They fight, and St. Clare, in attempting to part them, is stabbed.

"ST. CLARE had turned into a café to look over an evening paper. As he was reading, an affray arose between two gentlemen in the room who were both partially intoxicated. St. Clare and one or two others made an effort to separate them, and St. Clare received a fatal stab in the side with a bowie-knife, which he was attempting to wrest from one of them."—*Uncle Tom's Cabin.*

NOTE 30.—*Page* 258.

Yes, Mas'r, etc.

THE slave in the south calls the white man *master* whether he is *his* slave or not.

NOTE 31.—*Page* 265.

Oftentimes I have had feasts to which thousands gathered, etc.

WE will call attention to an occurrence of this kind which took place in Scotland in July, 1830, on the occasion of the *coming of age* of the son of a gentleman of large estate.

"The company took their seats at about two o'clock in the afternoon, and then commenced the cutting and distributing of the ox to which was added an unlimited supply of porter, strong ale, and whisky. *Four half-hogsheads of porter and six of strong ale, with about sixty gallons of beer, were provided for the occasion.* When the party had sufficiently regaled themselves, and had often devoted copious libations to the happiness of their generous employer and his amiable lady, they quietly dispersed. No sooner had they dispersed, than the spectators took possession of them, and the work of jollification went on briskly. Nor were the intoxicating draughts confined to those who encompassed the immense rustic table; pitchers of whisky mixed with strong ale and porter, were served out in the most liberal manner to all who chose to participate in them. The consequence was that in a very short time hundreds were in a state of deep intoxication; and hand-barrows and carts were instantly put in requisition to convey them to their several habitations. On the road from Bannockburn Muir, in every direction, people were found lying perfectly helpless. One man states, that between Bannockburn and Stirling, he loosened the neck-cloths, and placed in elevated positions, no less than eight individuals, evidently in danger of suffocation. But the scene around the table baffles description. Some ran thither to assist fathers — others to help sons — some to aid brothers — others to succor husbands — and not a few husbands to bring away frail wives. It frequently happened, too, that those who proffered assistance to others, were prevailed on to taste the liquor, and therefore were soon as much in need of aid themselves as those to whom they meant to extend it. Men, women, and children, were seen staggering about in inimitable confusion, tumbling over each other with the utmost unconcern, and lying by scores in every direction, neither able to tell their names nor their residences. On Sunday morning, parties were out in all directions looking for relations and friends, and removing them from the highways that they might not be observed by people going to church. No fewer than three individuals died from the effects of excessive drinking, not to mention several others who narrowly escaped a similar fate from the same cause, having been obliged to be repeatedly bled, and afterward attended by medical men. The three victims to this debauch were all stout young men in the prime of life." —*Public Papers*, (See Bacchus, by Grinrod.)

A work published in Scotland, entitled, " Some Account of the State of Morals and Religion in Syke, in 1805, and the Period immediately previous to It," had the following melancholy picture of the barbarous manner in which their funerals were conducted : " Some were free enough to acknowledge *that they experienced delight in hearing of the death of a man or woman, because of the prospect it afforded them of getting their fill of whisky.* The friends of the deceased were particularly anxious to solemnize the funeral with a great feast. This was what they called burying their deceased friend *with decency.* Hence they wasted, not only unnecessarily, but most wantonly, a great quantity of liquor and victuals on those occasions. This woful and barbarous practice was general and of so long standing, that persons, when arrived at old age, manifested a great anxiety to lay by a certain sum of money against their funeral. And upon their death-beds, while indifferent upon the state of their souls, they would not forget to order matters regarding their funerals; often expressing, that '*they would not be happy* unless men were drunk and fought at their funerals.' Their surviving relations would not forget to attend to their dying requests. For honor's sake this barbarous custom must be complied with. Not to do so, was incurring disgrace. Hence, many who were poor in circumstances, in order to attend it, ran themselves deeply into debt, which some of them were never able to discharge. Surely, it was a spectacle calculated to awaken deep regret in the bosom of an enlightened and benevolent Christian, to behold the distressed widow in the most destitute circumstances, going without shoes or head-dress, with six, seven, or eight ragged and starving children, while perhaps the only coin must be disposed of to procure whisky to make her neighbors drunk and fight one another. Although the people on other occasions would walk twenty or thirty miles without either food or drink, yet, at funerals the persons assembled must be treated to excess, though the place of interment should not be a mile distant. Scores of men must be invited; and every man served with four or even five glasses of strong whisky, and some food before they moved. Horse-loads of bread and cheese, dressed fowls, beef, and whisky, went along with them to the burying-ground. The funeral procession marched in good humor, preceded by a piper to the place of interment. When the grave was secured, they sat down in some convenient place in the open air, but not unfrequently in the church, when the minister happened to be *so generous* as to grant his permission. The feasting then commenced. The rulers of the feast were always most pressing in their liberality. A number of uninvited persons were seen to make their appearance; they were served separately. Bread and beef were tossed in the air that they might alight among the boys, to produce scuffling among them, to the no small amusement of the assembly, and the great honor of the deceased! As the drinking advanced, they became wildly obstreperous and tumultuous, so that the clamor might be heard at a great distance. When the day was far spent, and the excessive drinking of ardent spirits had produced general intoxication, fighting and bloodshed ensued. The men of the different clans would form themselves into parties, and furiously attack each other. Many would be so overcome with drunkenness, that, they could not move. The grosser the transactions of the day, it was considered the more *honorable*, and a more lasting monument to the memory of the deceased. At a gentleman's funeral five or six ankers of whisky would generally be consumed. Most of the ministers would countenance this barbarous custom with their presence, and none of them ever made any vigorous effort to suppress or abolish it."

In a work entitled "*The Life of the Empress Catherine*," we have the following dreadful account of a *gratuitous (?)* feast which occurred in the city of St. Petersburgh, Russia, in the year 1779: "One of the farmers of the brandy duty who had made an immense fortune by his contract, proposed to give a feast to the inhabitants of the city, in testimony of his gratitude to those who had enriched him. The victuals, the beer, and the brandy, which he caused to be served, cost him 20,000 rubles, — $15,000! The populace flocked in crowds to the place adjoining to the summer-garden, where he gave this enormous repast; and in spite of the precautions that had been taken, disturbances soon arose among this motley throng of guests. The contentions first began about the places, and the better kind of provisions spread upon the board; from struggles and noise they proceeded to blows. Several persons were killed; others became so intoxicated that they fell asleep in the streets and perished from the severity of the weather. The number of people who lost their lives on this occasion amounted to at least 500!"

NOTE 32.—*Page* 266.

Uncle Tom Beer, Uncle Tom Gin, Uncle Tom Wine, Uncle Tom Cogniac, and great many kinds.

DICKENS, in a graphic sketch of the bar of a large gin shop, tells us that "There are two side aisles of great casks, painted green and gold, enclosed within a light brass rail, and bearing such inscription as 'Old Tom, 549;' 'Young Tom, 360;' 'Samson, 1421.'"

Giving a general description of a gin-palace, the same author says, "A handsome plate of glass in one door directs you to the 'Counting-house;' another to the 'Bottle department;' a third to the 'Wholesale department;' a fourth to the 'Wine Promenade;' and so forth, until we are in daily expectation of meeting a 'Brandy Bell,' or a 'Whisky Entrance.' Then ingenuity is exhausted in devising attractive titles for the different descriptions of gin; and the dram-drinking portion of the community as they gaze upon the gigantic black and white announcements, which are only to be equalled in size by the figures beneath them, are left in a state of pleasing hesitation between 'The Cream of the Valley,' 'The Out and Out,' 'The no Mistake,' 'The Good for Mixing,' 'The real Knock-me-down,' 'The Celebrated Butter Gin,' 'The regular Flare-up,' and a dozen other equally inviting wholesome *liquors*. Although places of this description are to be met with in every second street, they are invariably numerous and splendid in precise proportion to the dirt and poverty of the surrounding neighborhood. The gin-shops in and near Drury-lane, Holborn, St. Giles's, Covent-Garden, and Clare-market, are the handsomest in London. There is more filth and misery near those great thoroughfares than in any other part of the city."

NOTE 33.— *Page* 266.

And thrash the ragged urchins till they smell.
Infernal power and answer with a yell.

THERE is doubtless no place in the world where human beings who are innocent of crime, receive such diabolical treatment as the servants in the British workshops do. It is a shocking subject of reflection — it is appalling; yet, to the effects of intemperance the cause of this cruelty can be generally traced. "In Sedgley they are sometimes struck with a red-hot iron, and burned and bruised simultaneously; sometimes they have a flash of lightning sent at them. When a bar of iron is drawn white-hot from the forge, it emits fiery particles, which the man commonly flings in a shower upon the ground by a swing of his arm, before placing the bar upon the anvil. This shower is sometimes directed at the boy. It may come over his hands and face, his naked arms, or on his breast. If his shirt be open in front, which is usually the case, the red-hot particles are lodged therein, and he has to shake them out."—HORNE, *Report*, p. 76, § 757.

"In Wednesbury, a few months ago an adult workman broke a boy's arm by a blow with a piece of iron; the boy went to school till his arm got well; his parents thought it a good opportunity to give him some schooling."—*Ib.*, *Evidence*, No. 331.

"The class of children in this district, the most abused and oppressed, are the apprentices, and particularly those who are bound to the small masters among the locksmiths, key and bolt makers, screw-makers, etc. Even among these small masters, there are respectable and humane men, who do not suffer any degree of poverty to render them brutal; but many of these men treat their apprentices not so much with neglect and harshness, as with ferocious violence, the result of unbridled passions, excited often by ardent spirits, acting on bodies exhausted by overwork, and on minds which have never received the slightest moral or religious culture, and which, therefore, never exercise the least moral or religious restraint."—*Ib.*

Though abundant is the evidence which is really startling to every one possessed of human feeling, I need here adduce only a few instances:

"—— ——, Aged sixteen: His master stints him from six in the morning till ten and sometimes eleven at night, as much as ever he can do; and if he don't do it his master gives him no supper, and gives him a good hiding, sometimes with a big strap, sometimes with a big stick. His master has cut his head open five times—once with a key, and twice with a lock; knocked the corner of a lock into his head twice—once with an iron bolt, and once with an iron shut—a thing that runs into the staple. His master's name is —— ——, of Little London. There is another apprentice besides him, who is treated just as bad."—*Ib.*, p. 32.

"—— ——, Aged fourteen: Has been an in-door apprentice three years. Has no wages; nobody gets any wages from him. Has to serve till he is twenty-one. His master behaves very bad. His mistress behaves worse, like a devil, she beats him; knocks his head against the wall. His master goes out a drinking, and when he comes back, if anything's gone wrong that he (the boy) knows nothing about, he is beat all the same."—*Ib.*, p. 32.

In the year 1831, a woman named Esther Hibner was executed in London for starving and beating to death a parish apprentice.—"The evidence in the case of Esther Hibner proved that a number of girls, pauper apprentices, were employed in a workshop; that their victuals consisted of garbage, commonly called hog's wash, and of this they never had enough to stay the pains of hunger; that they were kept half naked, half clothed in dirty rags, that they slept in a heap on the floor amid filth and stench; that they suffered dreadfully from cold; that they were forced to work so many hours together; that they used to fall asleep while at work; that for falling asleep, for not working as hard as their mistress wished, they were beaten with sticks, with fists, dragged by the hair, dashed on the ground, trampled upon and otherwise tortured; that they were found, all of them more or less, covered with chilblains, scurvy, bruises, and wounds; that one of them died of ill-treatment; and—mark this—that the discovery of that murder was made in consequence of the number of coffins which had issued from Esther Hibner's premises, and raised the curiosity of her neighbors. For this murder Mrs. Hibner was hanged; but what did she get for all the other murders which, referring to the number of coffins, we have a right to believe she committed. She got for each £10 ($50). That is to say, whenever she had worked, starved, beaten, dashed, and trampled a girl to death, she got another girl to treat in the same way with £10 for her trouble."—*England and America:* Harper & Brothers, publishers, 1834.

NOTE 34.—*Page* 270.

Uncle Tom was a saint and hated the good-vile drinks, etc.

UNCLE TOM thus warned his master of the consequences of intemperance:—"O, my dear young Mas'r! I'm afraid it will be *loss of all*—*all*—body and soul. The good book saith 'It biteth like a serpent and stingeth like an adder!' my dear Mas'r."—*Uncle Tom's Cabin.*

Note 35. — *Page* 272.

A gin-shop in England.

Dickens gives the following sketch of the bar of a large gin-shop and its ordinary customs in Drury-lane, London: "All is light and brilliancy. The hum of many voices issues from that splendid gin-shop, which forms the commencement of the two streets opposite, and the gay building with the fantastically ornamented parapet, the illuminated clock, the plate-glass windows, surrounded by stucco rosettes, and its profusion of gas-lights in richly gilt burners, is perfectly dazzling when contrasted with the darkness we have just left *(coming through the narrow streets and dirty courts which divide Drury-lane from Oxford-street, and that classical spot adjoining the brewery at the bottom of Tottendam-court-road, best known to the initiated as the Rookery).* The interior is even gayer than the exterior. A bar of French-polished mahogany, elegantly carved, extends the whole width of the place; and there are two side aisles of great casks, painted green and gold, enclosed within a light brass rail, and bearing such inscriptions as 'Old Tom, 549;' 'Young Tom, 360;' 'Samson, 1421.' Beyond the bar is a lofty and spacious saloon, full of the same enticing vessels, with a gallery running around it equally well furnished. On the counter in addition to the usual spirit apparatus, are two or three little baskets of cakes and biscuits, which are carefully secured at the top with wicker-work, to prevent their contents from being unlawfully extracted. Behind it are two showily-dressed damsels with large necklaces, dispensing the spirits and 'compounds.' They are assisted by the ostensible proprietor of the concern, a stout, coarse fellow in a fur cap, put on very much on one side, to give him a knowing air, and display his sandy whiskers to the best advantage. It is growing late and the throng of men, women, and children, who have been constantly going in and out, dwindle down to two or three occasional stragglers — cold, wretched-looking creatures in the last stage of emaciation and disease. That knot of Irish laborers at the lower end of the place, who have been alternately shaking hands with and threatening the life of each other for the last hour, become furious in their disputes, and finding it impossible to silence one man, who is particularly anxious to adjust the difference, they resort to the infallible expedient of knocking him down and jumping on him afterward. The man in the fur cap and the pot-boy rush out; a scene of riot and confusion ensues; half the Irishmen get shut out, and the other half get shut in; the pot-boy is knocked among the tubs in no time; the landlord hits everybody, and everybody hits the landlord; the barmaids scream; the police come in; and the rest in a confused mixture of arms, legs, staves, torn coats, shouting and struggling. Some of the party are borne off to the station-house, and the remainder slink home to beat their wives for complaining, and kick the children for daring to be hungry." And thus Dickens gives the description of the homes to which they slink: "Wretched houses with broken windows patched with rags, and paper, every room let out to a different family, and in many instances to two or even three; fruit and 'sweet-stuff' manufacturers in the cellars, barbers and red-herring venders in front parlors, and cobblers in the back; a bird-fancier on the first-floor, three families on the second, starvation in the attics, Irishmen in the passage; a 'musician' in the front kitchen, and a charwoman and five hungry children in the back one — filth everywhere — a gutter before the houses and a drain behind them — clothes drying and slops emptying from the windows; girls of fourteen or fifteen with matted hair, walking about barefooted, and in white great coats, almost their only covering; boys of all ages, in coats of all sizes and no coats at all; men and women, in every variety of scanty and dirty apparel, lounging, scolding, drinking, smoking, squabbling, fighting, and swearing."

NOTE 36.—*Page* 298.

—— But now I can not feel
My body with my hands.

A CERTAIN individual, in describing the manner in which he had been afflicted with delirium tremens, says: "I lost the sense of feeling too; for I attempted to grasp my arm in one hand, but consciousness was gone. I put my hand to my side, to my head, but felt nothing; and still I knew that my limbs and frame were there."

THE END.

www.ingramcontent.com/pod-product-compliance
Lightning Source LLC
LaVergne TN
LVHW020128110826
845151LV00001B/307